D1029650

**Urban Growth
in the
Nonmetropolitan
South**

Urban Growth in the Nonmetropolitan South

Leonard F. Wheat

Lexington Books
D.C. Heath and Company
Lexington, Massachusetts
Toronto

Library of Congress Cataloging in Publication Data

Wheat, Leonard F
    Urban growth in the nonmetropolitan South.

    1. Urbanization—Southern States.   2. Southern States
—Population.   3. Cities and Towns—Growth.   4. Indus-
tries, Location of—Southern States.   5. Economic develop-
ment. I. Title.
HT123.5.S6W47   301.36'3'0975   76-24966
ISBN 0-669-00964-4

Published simultaneously in Canada

Printed in the United States of America

International Standard Book Number: 0-669-00964-4

Library of Congress Catalog Card Number: 76-24966

To my parents
   Leonard B. Wheat
   Gertrude Wieland Wheat

Contents

List of Tables and Figures

Tables

Preface

The rising interest in urban economics underscores a need for better knowledge of urban growth, particularly in the nonmetropolitan sector, where federal and state economic development efforts are concentrated. Why do some nonmetropolitan cities grow faster than others? How can we tell whether a city is likely to grow fast in the future?

Cross-sectional statistical analysis is an approach well suited to exploring these questions. Yet, quite surprisingly, the literature has almost nothing to offer in terms of research that compares growth with a broad spectrum of other community characteristics for a cross-section of nonmetropolitan cities. The most comprehensive studies, in terms of sample size and variables tested, have not looked directly at cities at all; they have looked at counties or multicounty areas. But counties are not cities, and most county data are not adequate substitutes for data on the cities within those counties. County *growth* data are particularly hazardous, because population decline in the rural parts of a county may give a distorted picture of what is happening in the urban part. Another limitation is that some cross-sectional studies, though well designed for the framework of their own special objectives, focus on just one or a few relationships—for example, that between population and growth rate. This problem has been compounded by the inclusion of metropolitan suburbs in a sample. This makes it impossible to isolate the effects of local influences from those belonging to nearby cities or to a metropolitan area as a whole. Other studies have been relatively superficial, using samples of less than twenty cities. Their findings are stimulating but not statistically significant.

The present study avoids these limitations. It uses city rather than county data, except for two variables available only on a county basis. It examines most of the leading hypotheses, slighting only those that are not amenable to testing with available data. It uses only nonmetropolitan cities. (These range from 5,000 to 50,000 in population.) And it employs fairly large samples: the principal sample has 116 cities, while three secondary ones have considerably more.

The study is also designed to control other factors that might bias the findings. Regional causes of variation in local growth rates are minimized by limiting the study to one region (the South), by providing subordinate analyses for two subregions (Southeast and Southwest), by holding state and dummy subregional variables constant, and by comparing "fast" and "slow" subsamples having the same geographic stratification. The potential influence of a neighboring city on a sample city's growth is controlled by using a gravity formula to eliminate from the four samples those cities deemed too close to their neighbors. Partial correlations, used to hold anywhere from one to a comprehensive set of significant variables constant, reduce the chances that one factor's link with growth is really due to variation in a third factor.

The findings, I think, will be of special interest to students of industrial location. True, the study looks broadly at population growth rather than narrowly at manufacturing growth. But most population growth seems to stem from manufacturing stimuli, and most of the tests involve factors (e.g., transportation) that influence plant location. Many findings have no plausible explanation other than one supplied by an industrial location hypothesis.

In interpreting the findings and formulating conclusions, I have tried to consider all the possibilities—direct causation, reverse causation, proxy relationships, and so on. The conclusions of other studies, including interview and questionnaire studies of plant location decisions, have been helpful in this respect. Partial correlation and other diagnostic tests have contributed to appraisals of suspected proxy relationships. And of course theory, including theoretical analysis of competing but not equally plausible explanatory hypotheses, has had an important role.

Still, a conclusion that the relationship between growth and some other local variable is or is not causal is ultimately a judgment. No doubt my judgment is wrong in places. I can only hope that these errors will be recognized and will lead others to formulate better tests and better explanations. Meanwhile, even a misinterpreted finding may be useful to a practitioner looking for better indicators for predicting growth.

**Urban Growth
in the
Nonmetropolitan
South**

1

Introduction

This study compares fast-growing and slow-growing nonmetropolitan cities in thirteen southern states. Looking at 1960–70 population growth rates, it seeks (1) to determine the causes of fast and slow growth, (2) to find statistical indicators of growth potential, and (3) to use these indicators in formulas that predict "fast" or "slow" growth. Knowledge in these areas can contribute to wise geographic planning decisions and to a variety of forecasting needs. It can be particularly useful for economic development planning, which requires the selection of growth centers and the evaluation of competing projects proposed for different places. The study uses chi-square, correlation, and other statistical tests to explore many hypotheses. It identifies sixteen factors that are significantly related to growth; air service ranks highest. The factors enter into two formulas. Tested with the original data, the formulas correctly classify 56 of 58 Southeast cities and 56 of 58 Southwest cities.

Objectives and Scope

The federal government, regional organizations, and states are engaged in economic development planning. The federal and regional planners try to assist economically distressed areas. State efforts are more broadly geared to achieving higher growth rates. State planners may also attempt to shape the geographical pattern of growth (directive planning), or they may simply try to provide needed facilities in places where growth is expected (nondirective planning).

Whatever orientation the planning may have, planners need to know what causes growth and how to predict it. This knowledge can facilitate sound decisions on growth centers if, and to the extent that, high growth potential is to be a major criterion for growth center designation. It can also facilitate project decisions by showing which places are viable enough to be likely to respond to proposed public works projects. And—of special interest to state planners (not to mention market analysts)—this knowledge can indicate where new public (or business) facilities will probably be needed to accommodate rapid growth.

The study's scope is limited to the South. For purposes of this study, the South is a thirteen-state region: Virginia, North and South Carolina, Georgia, Florida, Kentucky, Tennessee, Alabama, Mississippi, Arkansas, Louisiana, Oklahoma, and Texas. A nationwide study would have been too big to handle. Equally important, regional factors affecting city growth would have been

1

relatively difficult to control in a nationwide study. This problem is potentially serious where regional effects—the effect of geographic location on local effects—are concerned. Some local influences are related to growth only in certain regions, or else have different (even opposite) relationships to growth in different regions. Broadening the regional scope of the analysis makes it difficult, sometimes impossible, to detect such relationships.

The South was chosen as the study region primarily because it is fast-growing. Experience has shown that factors allocating a region's growth among cities are hard to identify statistically in regions where there is little growth to allocate, as in the Manufacturing Belt. Another consideration is that the South, compared to the even faster growing West, has far more cities and can provide larger samples. Finally, the South has a disproportionate share of the nation's distressed areas. Findings about the South therefore have wider application in economic development.

The study's scope is also limited to nonmetropolitan cities in the 5,000 to 50,000 population range. Metropolitan cities were excluded because their growth may be influenced more by the growth or other characteristics of the metropolitan area as a whole than by their own features. Metropolitan suburbs and satellites could seriously distort any findings concerning relationships between growth and other factors. Suburban growth is especially hazardous for a study exploring population's relationship to growth. As for the central cities— cities above 50,000—they could be examined realistically only by treating a central city and its suburbs as a single entity; the clerical burden would be prohibitive.

Clerical constraints are partly responsible for the 5,000 population minimum. But a minimum was also necessary to avoid overloading the samples with small and possibly nonviable towns whose growth charcteristics could differ radically from those of larger cities. Moreover, some data are not available for cities below 10,000, and almost nothing is available for those below 2,500. The 5,000 and 10,000 cutoffs accord with what some observers think are ordinarily reasonable minimums for growth center designation.

Also eliminated were nonmetropolitan cities lacking adequate separation— defined by formula—from other cities located nearby. This was done for essentially the same reasons that metropolitan cities were eliminated: to ensure that sample city growth was not unduly influenced by assets or liabilities (e.g., labor force or manufacturing) of other cities.

General Findings

The study's findings support 16 of 23 hypotheses tested. Among the factors found to be significantly related to growth, air service looks strongest. Unemployment, prior growth, colleges, highways, property taxes, wages, existing manufacturing, metropolitan area proximity, and racial mix round out a list of the ten most important factors. Some factors are significant only in the Southeast or the Southwest. Most of these cases stem from the relatively labor-intensive structure of southeastern manufacturing, which contrasts with a capital-intensive structure found in the Southwest. Not all of the significant relationships are causal; some factors, such as prior growth, are good indicators because they reflect others that may not be directly measurable.

2 Methodology

The study methodology revolves around a comparison of the characteristics of fast-growing cities with those of slow-growing ones; it also involves comparing growth rates for cities in different population intervals. The fast-slow comparisons use chi-square and correlation (including partial and multiple correlation) tests to measure relationships between growth and numerous other factors, while the population-interval analysis uses a t test to compare growth rates. The basic measure of growth is 1960-70 percentage increase in population. But most of the correlation tests entail a form of discriminant analysis using a dummy (fast-slow) growth variable. These tests compare the fastest one-third and the slowest one-third (equal numbers) of each state's cities. The comparisons employ both regional variables, used for tighter control over geographic influences, and local variables, which represent twenty-three hypotheses. Standardized control sets—fixed combinations of variables held constant—support partial correlation tests that seek to discover hidden relationships and to verify apparently significant ones.

Sampling Procedure

The study uses three samples:[a] a fast-slow sample of cities above 10,000, a fast-slow sample of cities above 5,000, and a population-interval sample of cities above 5,000. The over-10,000 sample also has an expanded version, referred to hereafter as the *augmented sample,* which includes cities with moderate growth rates (middle one-third); so in a sense there are four samples. The sampling procedure involved (1) screening out unusable cities, (2) preparing the fast-slow samples, and (3) preparing the population-interval sample.

---

[a]These are not random samples but groups of cities. Random (or otherwise representative) samples are required when a population parmeter is to be estimated from a sample statistic—as when the average age of all workers in a city is to be estimated from a sample. But random samples are neither necessary not desirable where two or more groups are being compared in the study of a relationship. In this case, random samples would often cause the groups to be dissimilar with respect to factors that could bias the findings. For instance, in a comparison of cancer rates between smokers and nonsmokers, random samples of each group would practically guarantee a larger proportion of men among the smokers than in the nonsmoking group.

Screening. All cities in the thirteen states were first screened to eliminate those below 5,000 in population and those located in SMSA (Standard Metropolitan Statistical Area) counties. The latter group, of course, included all cities above 50,000—the minimum population for SMSA designation—as well as all suburbs and satellites.

Next, other cities similarly located too close to neighboring ones were screened out. Minimum required separation was determined by the formula $D = \sqrt[4]{P_n}$, where D is the minimum allowable separation (miles) between cities and P_n is the population of the nearby city. To pass, a city had to be at least ten miles from another city of 10,000, fourteen miles from a city of 50,000, and twenty-two miles from a city of 250,000. A usable city could thus still be fairly close to an SMSA central city. This was intentional: the formula sought to eliminate the strongest effects of proximity without making it difficult to evaluate the hypothetical effect of SMSAs on growth in their hinterlands.

Another type of screening was aimed at unique attractions, mostly in Florida, that might bias the findings. Florida is the land of retirement havens, Disney World, and Cape Canaveral. Boom growth in or near these places could obscure the relationships being studied. Places known to be or suspected of being (coastal cities) retirement havens were therefore eliminated. Places close enough to Disney World and Cape Canaveral to be bedroom communities for them were likewise dropped. Williamsburg, Virginia; Daytona Beach, Florida; and Hot Springs, Arkansas, were also eliminated because of unusual growth-generating characteristics.

Fast-Slow Samples. The two fast-slow samples were obtained by ranking the remaining cities by 1960–70 population growth rate. This was done state by state, but with Texas being treated as three "states" (East, South, and West). Approximately the top and bottom thirds from each state went into the samples. Fewer cities were used where necessary to provide at least (*a*) a 10 percent difference—say, 14.6 percent compared to 4.6 percent—between the slowest "fast" and fastest "slow" city in a *state* and (*b*) a 2 percent difference—8 percent compared to 6 percent in the over-10,000 sample—between the slowest "fast" and fastest "slow" city in the entire *sample*.

Each state provided as many fast cities as slow ones. This was necessary to control subregional geographic influences—resources, markets, and the like—that might otherwise distort the findings: it would not do to have most of the slow cities concentrated in Atlantic Coast states and most of the fast ones in the Southwest. The equal-numbers rule means that the fast and slow subsamples have about the same geographic distribution.

The average growth rate for the fast cities in the over-10,000 sample was 29 percent. The average for the slow cities was –7 percent.

The augmented version of the over-10,000 sample included cities with moderate growth rates taken from the middle third of the array. Each state contributed as many moderate as fast (also slow) cities. Whereas the basic sample (fast-slow) was designed for tests using an orthodox 1–0 dummy variable, the augmented sample (fast-moderate-slow) was for tests with a 2–1–0 dummy. It also provided a larger sample on which to base tests in which actual percentage growth was the dependent variable. The average growth rate for the moderate cities was 7 percent.

For analytical purposes, the samples were divided into *Southeast* (Virginia, the Carolinas, Georgia, Florida, Kentucky, Tennesse, and Alabama) and *Southwest* (Mississippi, Arkansas, Louisiana, Oklahoma, and Texas). The numbers of cases in the regional and overall samples were as follows:

Region	*Basic* *Over 10,000*	*Augmented* *Over 10,000*	*Over 5,000*
Southeast	58	87	140
Southwest	58	87	120
Overall South	116	174	260

The over-5,000 sample includes some cities above 10,000 that are not in the over-10,000 sample. And the over-10,000 sample has some cities that are not in the over-5,000 sample. Thus, despite considerable overlap, the samples have more independence from each other than provided by the mere inclusion of cities of 5,000 to 10,000 in the over-5,000 sample.

In order to provide the over-10,000 sample with at least three fast and three slow cities from each state (except Florida), the largest slow city in the 9,000s was added to the Tennessee cities. This was balanced by a fast city in the 9,000 range from Georgia, where fast cities were scarce.

Population-Interval Sample. The last sample is for comparing growth rates of different sized cities. This requires a new type of geographic comparability—not between fast and slow groups, but between cities in different population intervals. Comparability was achieved by having each state contribute to each of five intervals as many cities as a 12:4:2:2:2 ratio allowed. This ratio calls for twelve cities of 5,000 to 9,999, four of 10,000 to 14,999, two of 15,000 to 19,999, two of 20,000 to 29,999, and two of 30,000 to 49,999. Two states each gave 1.5 times the basic ratio; Florida had too few usable cities for even an 0.5 share and was left out; the other states each contributed twenty-two cities.

Where a state had more than enough cities for an interval, random sampling was generally used. But in the two highest intervals, random procedures were combined with stratification. The fourth interval was subdivided into 20,000 to 24,999 and 25,000 to 29,999. The fifth was subdivided into 30,000 to 39,999 and 40,000 to 49,999. If a state had no cities in a certain subinterval, the nearest (in population) city from the second subinterval was used; if the subinterval had just one city, it was used; and if the subinterval had more than one city (after any loans to the other subinterval), a random-number selection was made.

Five states could not meet the ratio for one or two intervals. For these intervals, dummy cities were created to preserve geographic comparability. A dummy city's growth rate was computed as the average of (1) the state's median growth rate for all cities that survived screening, (2) the growth rates for the available cities in the dummy's interval, counted individually, (3) the median growth rate for all cities in the state's next higher population interval, and (4) the median for the next lower interval. This procedure allows a dummy city to reflect the average growth rate for its state while giving greater weight to cities near the dummy's interval and greatest weight to cities actually in that interval. The dummies thus preserve geographic comparability among the sample's intervals (by reflecting the state median) without ignoring growth rate differences among different-sized cities. Ten of 330 sample cities are dummies.

(When differences between mean growth rates were tested for significance, the dummy cities were used to compute means but not standard deviations, standard errors, or degrees of freedom; the dummies were not allowed to reduce the amount of dispersion—which the averaging procedure would otherwise do—or to artifically inflate N. The result is a higher standard error, a lower N, and therefore a more conservative test of significance.)

Hypotheses and Variables

The study tests many hypotheses. These postulate that growth is related—not necessarily causally—to (1) population, (2) business importance, (3) trade importance, (4) manufacturing levels, (5) air service, (6) Interstate System highways, (7) water transportation, (8) colleges and universities, (9) schooling, (10) wage levels, (11) skilled labor supplies, (12) property taxes, (13) distances to major SMSAs, (14) the populations of these SMSAs, (15) the growth rates of these SMSAs, (16) gravity relationships involving interaction among the three preceding factors, (17) racial mix, (18) residential amenities, (19) health and medical services, (20) hospitals, (21) prior growth, (22) prior net migration, and (23) the unemployment rate. Testing these hypotheses requires the use of dependent variables (measuring growth), subregional independent variables (for holding extraneous factors constant), and local independent variables (representing the hypotheses).

Dependent Variables. There are three dependent variables. All use population to measure growth. Population growth is used because it avoids many problems that go with alternative measures. Manufacturing employment data, for example, are not published for many small cities and for those with disclosure problems; are sometimes distorted by strikes, recessions, and reclassifications; and do not record nonmanufacturing growth. True, city population growth figures are weakened by annexations. Most southern cities have annexations, so these cases cannot be eliminated without destroying most of the sample. However, as explained in detail in the next chapter, annexations do not seriously undermine the validity of the data.

The three dependent variables are the city's 1960–70 population growth rate and two dummy variables based on the growth rate. These variables and their abbreviations are as follows:

Variable	Description
GRO-%	1960–70 percentage growth in population.
GRO-2:1:0	Growth dummy, where 2 = fast, 1 = moderate, and 0 = slow.
GRO-2:0	Growth dummy, where 2 = fast, 0 = slow, and moderate cities are excluded from the sample. (A 2–0 dummy–equivalent to a 1–0 dummy multiplied by the constant 2–always gives the same correlations as a conventional 1–0 dummy, hence in effect *is* a 1–0 dummy.)

Tests using GRO-% with the over-10,000 sample used the augmented version of the sample. This increased the number of cases behind the correlations. GRO-2:1:0, used only with the over-10,000 sample, did not perform as well as the other two dependent variables. It was dropped after preliminary testing and will not be discussed further. The other dummy, GRO-2:0, proved very successful and became the principal dependent variable. Its success probably results mainly from the improved control it provides over geographic (regional) factors. Whereas GRO-% tends to be high or low according to whether or not a state is fast-growing, GRO-2:0 is not affected by state growth rates: "fast" and "slow" are defined by *state* norms, with each state contributing exactly as many fast as slow cities to the sample.

Subregional Independent Variables. Since GRO-% is affected by state growth rates and by the geographic factors behind them, correlations between GRO-% and local independent variables can be distorted by geographic factors. (In general, the geographic factors will tend to hide significant relationships, making the correlations lower than they should be.) To control this distortion, seven subregional independent variables–geographic variables–were used. These, along with other independent variables, were held constant in partial correlation tests. The subregional variables:

Variable	Description
ST-%P	State 1960–70 percentage increase in population–the median for cities left after screening, including those not used.
ST-%M	State 1958–67 percentage increase in manufacturing employment.
SE-SW	Southeast-Southwest dummy, where 1 = Southeast and 0 = Southwest.
COAST	East Coast dummy, where 1 = Virginia, the Carolinas, Georgia, and Florida and 0 = all other states.
DELTA	Delta states dummy, where 1 = Mississippi, Arkansas, and Louisiana and 0 = all other states.

Variable	Description
W-TEX	West Texas dummy, where 1 = any of 113 West Texas counties (ultraslow growth) and 0 = all other counties and states.
ISOL	Spatial isolation semidummy, valuing states according to distance from the Manufacturing Belt: 0 = Virginia and Kentucky; 1 = the Carolinas and Tennessee; 2 = Georgia, Alabama, Mississippi, and Arkansas; 3 = Florida, Louisiana, and eastern Oklahoma; 4 = East Texas and western Oklahoma; and 5 = South and West Texas.

All cities from the same state (or substate) have the same value for each subregional variable. Each dummy represents the net effect of all subregional influences explaining the difference between the growth rate central tendency for that subregion and the central tendency for outside cities. ISOL reflects a known tendency for manufacturing to grow faster as the "distance tariff" protecting new plants from Manufacturing Belt competition increases. All seven subregional variables naturally have simple correlations of .00 with GRO-2 : 0— because each state has as many fast as slow cities, which means that the fast and slow groups have identical value distributions for these variables.

Local Independent Variables. The local independent variables value each city according to its own—rather than subregional—characteristics. Over two hundred of these independent variables were tested. Most were functions (squares, logs, reciprocals, dummies, and so on) of one or another of twenty-six basic variables. The basic variables, numbered according to the previously enumerated hypotheses, are listed here.

Variable	Description
*1. POP	Population, 1960. (Source: U.S. Bureau of the Census, *1970 Census of Population,* series PC[1]-A, state reports, table 6.)
*2. BUSNS	Rand McNally business importance rating: 1 = nationally important business center, 2 = regional business center, 3 = important local business center, 4 = other local business center, and 5 = unrated. (This and the next two variables have no ratings for most cities below 15,000 and for almost all below 10,000.) (Source: Rand McNally, *City Rating Guide.*)
*3. TRADE	Rand McNally trade rating, where 4 = major primary basic trading center, 3 = other primary basic trading center, 2 = secondary basic trading center, 1 = local business center, and 0 = unrated. (Source: Rand McNally, *City Rating Guide.*)
*4a. MFG	Rand McNally manufacturing rating, converted to numerical values from published upper-lower case (primary-secondary) letter codes: 3 = Mm, 2 = Mx, 1 = Xm, and 0 = Xx or unrated, where M is manufacturing and X is any other economic activity. (Source: Rand McNally, *City Rating Guide.*)
4b. VA/P	1958 manufacturing value added per 1960 capita. (Source: Computed from VA and POP. VA taken from U.S. Bureau of the Census, *1958 Census of Manufactures,* vol. 3, state reports, table 3.)
4c. E_m/E	Manufacturing employment as a percentage of total employment, 1960. (Source: U.S. Bureau of the Census, *1960 Census of Population,* series PC[1]-C, state reports, table 33.)
*5. AIR	Air service: distance in road miles from city center to nearest airport

	with certificated air service. (Sources: airline route maps and road maps.)
*6. HWY	Highways: distance in road miles to nearest Interstate System inter-change. (Source: road maps.)
*7. WATER	Waterway dummy: 2 = cities on navigable inland and coastal water-ways 9 or more feet deep, 1 = cities on waterways under 9 feet deep, and 0 = nonwaterway cities. (Source: American Waterways Opera-tors, Inc., inland waterways map.)
*8. COL-5	College-university rating: 5 = state university, 4 = any other school granting Ph.D.'s, 3 = master's degree school with at least 2,000 students, 2 = smaller master's degree school or bachelor's degree school with at least 1,000 students, 1 = smaller bachelor's degree school with at least 500 students or junior college, and 0 = anything else. (Based on U.S. Office of Education, *Education Directory*, 1965.)
9a. HI-SCH	Percentage of high school graduates for persons 25 years old and over. (Source: U.S. Bureau of the Census, *1960 Census of Popula-tion*, series PC[1]-C, state reports, table 32. HI-SCH was converted to a 0-to-9 scale by subtracting 25 and dividing by 5.)
9b. SCHOOL	Percentage in school for persons 14 to 17 years old. (Source: U.S. Bureau of the Census, *1960 Census of Population*, Series PC[1]-C, table 32.)
10. EARN	Median annual earnings, operatives and kindred workers, male, 1960—a wage proxy. (Source: U.S. Bureau of the Census, *1960 Census of Population*, series PC[1]-C, state reports, table 76.)
11. SKILL	Craftsmen, foremen, and kindred workers, 1960—a proxy for skilled labor. (Source: U.S. Bureau of the Census, *1960 Census of Popula-tion*, series PC[1]-C, state reports, table 74.)
12. TAX/P	1962 property taxes per capita, county (amounts over $99 recorded as $99). (Source: U.S. Bureau of the Census, *County and City Data Book*, 1967, table 2.)
*13. D_m	Distance in road miles to the SMSA of 250,000 or more that is either closest or not over 50 miles farther than the closest and has a higher P_m/D_m^2, where P_m is the "metro" population. (Source: road maps.)
*14. P_m	1960 population of the SMSA defined above, as delineated in the 1970 census. (Source: U.S. Bureau of the Census, *1970 Census of Population*, series PC[1]-A, state reports, table 13.)
*15. G_m	1960–70 percentage growth in population for the same SMSA. (Source: U.S. Bureau of the Census, *1970 Census of Population*, series PC[1]-A, state reports, table 13.)
*16. P_mG_m/D_m	A representative gravity variable, one of fifteen tested.
*17. RACE	Population percentage nonwhite, 1960. (Source: U.S. Bureau of the Census, *1960 Census of Population*, series PC[1]-C, state reports, table 13.)
18. PROF/P	Male professional, technical, and kindred workers per capita—a speculative proxy for residential and cultural amenities. (Based on U.S. Bureau of the Census, *1960 Census of Population*, series PC[1]-C, state reports, table 74.)
19. MED/P	Self-employed male medical and other health workers per capita—a proxy for medical services. (Source: U.S. Bureau of the Census, *1960 Census of Population*, series PC[1]-C, state reports, table 74.)
20. HOSP	Total hospital employees, 1960. (Source: U.S. Bureau of the Census, *1960 Census of Population*, series PC[1]-C, state reports, table 75.)
21. G:50–60	1950–60 population growth rate (rates above 50 percent recorded as 50, rates below –9 percent recorded as –9). (Source: U.S. Bureau of the Census, *1960 Census of Population*, series PC[1]-A, state reports, table 5.)

Variable	Description
22. MIGR	1950–60 net migration, county (city figures not available). (Source: U.S. Bureau of the Census, *County and City Data Book, 1967*, table 2.)
23. UNEMP	Percent unemployed, 1960 (rates above 9 percent recorded as 9 percent). (Source: U.S. Bureau of the Census, *1960 Census of Population*, series PC[1]-C, state reports, table 33.)

Only the variables preceded by an asterisk (*) were used with the over-5,000 sample. This limitation reflects workload considerations and the unavailability of some data for cities under 10,000.

Standardized Control Sets

Much of the study involves partial correlations—correlations that create an "other factors being equal" situation by statistically holding one or more variables constant. (Simple correlations hold nothing constant.) The most important "partials" are those based on *standarized control sets.* These are combinations (sets) of variables that simultaneously hold constant (control) a comprehensive set of factors. There is one set for the Southeast, one for the Southwest, and one for the overall South. Each set has one variable for each factor found to be significant in the corresponding region. It also has another variable or two representing factors that are significant in another region and approach significance in the control set's region. And it includes two or three regional variables that help compensate for geographic unevenness in the relationships between the other independent variables and growth.

    The control sets are standardized in the sense that, in most of the study's partial correlation tests for a given region, the same control variables are used. Each independent variable is thus placed on the same footing for comparative purposes.

    The three standardized control sets used with the over-10,000 sample vis-à-vis GRO-2 : 0 follow. With two exceptions, variables on the same line describe the same factor, although the variables used to measure that factor may differ. The factors controlled are (1, 2) subregional characteristics, (3) the negative side of manufacturing, or slow growth tendencies in cities that have manufacturing, (4a) the positive side of manufacturing, or the proportionality of growth to manufacturing where capital-intensive industry exists, (4b) schooling, which seems to be a proxy for skilled labor and other urban characteristics, (5) air service, (6) Interstate System highways, (7) colleges, (8) property taxes, (9) wage levels, (10) racial mix, (11) prior growth, (12) prior unemployment, (13) distance to the nearest metropolitan area, and (14) population-weighted growth rate of the nearest major metropolitan area. The second variable on the last line (SE-SW) is an extra subregional variable. The control sets:

	Southeast	*Southwest*	*South*
1.	COAST	W-TEX	COAST
2.	ISOL	ISOL	W-TEX
3.	MFG > 0	MFG > 0	MFG > 0
4.	MFG	SCHOOL	MFG
5.	AIR > 30	AIR > 25	AIR > 25
6.	1/logHWY(0.8)	HWY > 8	SE-SW/HWY
7.	COL-3	√COL-3	√COL-3
8.	TAX/P ⩾ 40	TAX/P	TAX/P ⩾ 40
9.	EARN	EARN	EARN ⩾ 3¼:3
10.	RACE ⩾ 33	RACE ⩾ 20	RACE ⩾ 33:20
11.	G:50–60	G:50–60	G:50–60
12.	UNEMP ⩾ 4	UNEMP ⩾ 4	UNEMP ⩾ 5:4
13		D_m > 160	SW × D_m > 160
14.		$P_m G_m$	SE-SW

Some of these variables are derived from the basic variables introduced earlier. Nine are 1–0 dummy variables valued at one where the basic variable is greater than (>) or else greater than or equal to (⩾) an indicated value. (Throughout this study, the "greater than" and "greater than or equal to" signs always depict dummy variables.) EARN ⩾ 3¼ : 3, RACE ⩾ 33 : 20, and UNEMP ⩾ 5 : 4 are 2–1–0 dummies valued at two where the basic variable's value equals or exceeds the value before the colon and at zero where the basic value is less than the value following the colon, except that with EARN ⩾ 3¼ : 3 the 3¼ represents $3,250 and the 3 stands for $3,000. The third highway variable, essentially SE-SW × 1/HWY, equals 1/HWY in the Southeast (where highways are quite significant) and 0/HWY, or zero, in the Southwest. COL-3 is valued at three for Ph.D. schools, two for master's degree schools, one for four-year colleges, and zero for anything else. SW × D_m > 160 is D_m > 160 multiplied by a 1–0 Southwest-Southeast dummy, which means that all Southeast cases (in addition to most Southwest ones) are valued at zero.

The four subregional variables (e.g., COAST) do not actually control subregional influences when used with GRO-2 : 0. Rather, they compensate for geographic differences in other relationships. Starting with simple correlations of .00, they become positive or negative only after other variables begin to overcompensate or undercompensate in certain states for the local factors controlled.

When MFG and MFG > 0 are used in combination (as in the Southeast) and are opposite in sign, they jointly describe a U-shaped curve relating manufacturing to growth. Where MFG > 0 is used alone (Southwest), a negative relationship between manufacturing and growth is described.

Two exceptions occur to the rule that the standardized partials put all variables on the same footing. First, any variable belonging to a standardized control set is excluded when its partial or that of a closely related variable is computed: one cannot measure a factor's relationship to growth when that factor is held constant. Second, and for similar reasons, one or both economic variables (lines 11 and 12) are exluded whenever they appear to duplicate a variable being tested. G : 50–60 and the UNEMP dummies are assumed to be, in part, proxies for another independent variable when that other variable's partial is reduced by holding the economic variable constant.

3

Findings: Preliminary Matters

The findings concerning relationships between the independent variables and growth are presented in following chapters. First, however, we must take up some preliminary matters. These involve (1) the effect of annexations on the findings, (2) the scope of the presentation, (3) significance levels, (4) correlations involving the seven geographic variables, and (5) intercorrelations among the independent variables.

The Effect of Annexations

The population growth figures used in this and many other studies include annexed territory. That is, the 1970 but not the 1960 populations include areas annexed during the decade by the cities studied. There is no satisfactory way to avoid the problem. If the annexed populations are subtracted from the 1970 population, the potentially most significant element of growth—fringe area growth outside the 1960 city limits—is lost. If one tries to increase the 1960 base by the 1960 population of subsequently annexed areas, one finds that 1960 annexed-area population is unavailable. If cities with annexations are left out, few cities remain, because most cities (at least southern cities in the 10,000 to 50,000 range) had annexations. Alternative measures of growth are sometimes inappropriate and always have their own problems—for example, the problem of using county data to explore growth that belongs essentially to cities. Population growth data, annexations included, therefore continue to be used. Does this seriously vitiate findings and conclusions based on these data? The following analysis concludes that the problem is not serious.

The Berry-Lamb-Gillard Critique. Apprehension about the effect of annexations on the validity of growth data is fairly common. Take, for example, a recent attack on U.S. Department of Agriculture findings that around two hundred nonmetropolitan cities of 10,000 to 50,000 population grew by 15 percent or more during the 1960s.[1] In an appendix to a study by Brian Berry, Berry's assistants Lamb and Gillard argue that the USDA findings are "totally inadequate" from a growth center perspective.[2] A major reason is that a large share of the population growth came from annexations. Since the Berry-Lamb-Gillard analysis has the most thoroughly articulated arguments to be found against using annexed areas in measuring population growth, it deserves careful evaluation.

15

The Department contended that the two-hundred-odd cities grew fast enough—15 percent or more—during the 1960s to serve as growth centers for rural development purposes. The authors challenge this contention. Much of their challenge relates to the idea that annexations distorted the Department's growth statistics. The Berry-Lamb-Gillard critique raises four main arguments purporting to show that annexations invalidate the 1960–70 growth rates used by the Department:

1. Some of the annexed-area populations were already there in 1960 and do not represent new growth.
2. Population growth for the 1960 (before annexation) areas was sometimes negative and was 15 percent or more in only 30 percent of the cities.
3. Employment growth figures contradict the Department's population growth figures by showing that
    (a) 1963–67 absolute growth in manufacturing employment for the counties involved was sometimes negative and was under 1,000 in 70 percent of the cases, and
    (b) 1950–60 overall employment growth for the counties—and probably, therefore, 1960–70 growth too—was mainly due to above-national-average growth rates in nationally slow or declining industries.
4. About 16 percent of the cities neither (a) had population growth of more than 5 percent for their 1960 census areas nor (b) were located in counties that exceeded the national growth rate of 13 percent.

Flaws in the Critique. The Berry-Lamb-Gillard arguments and evidence concerning the effect of annexations are seriously deficient. We can begin with the first argument, holding that some of the annexed population does not represent new growth. Whether or not counting the people previously living in an area annexed after 1960 seriously distorts 1960–70 growth rates depends on two things: (1) whether a large percentage of total "growth," including growth of the original 1960 area, is made up of 1960 residents of the annexed area and (2) if so, whether those 1960 residents are appreciably offset by uncounted new residents living in unannexed fringe areas. Regarding the first point, suppose a city with a 1960 population of 10,000 grew by 20 percent, or 2,000 people, consisting of 500 within the original boundaries, a 1,000 increase in an annexed area, and 500 previously living in the annexed area. Legitimate growth is still 15 percent. And maybe more. For what about the new subdivision and other fringe growth that was there in 1970 but not annexed until 1971? In some situations, uncounted fringe growth will actually exceed the pre-1960 growth that was counted.

The authors' second argument, citing slow growth in many of the original areas, implies that original-area statistics are as reliable as statistics that include annexed areas. Thus the authors argue that "in only about 38 percent of the centers did population increase exceed the national average when considering changes only in the 1960 census area."[3] This argument ignores the customary nature of growth. Particularly in the larger cities, original areas tend to be relatively built up. Growth therefore goes to fringe areas. In time, and sometimes immediately, the fringe areas are annexed. Ignoring this growth can mean ignoring the major element of growth.

The next argument uses 1963–67 absolute increases in county manufacturing employment to supposedly contradict 1960–70 percentage increases in city population. This curious effort displays five analytical errors. First, the 1963–67 period covers only four of the ten years covered in the population growth rates. The manufacturing growth figures would have to be multiplied by 2.5 to get even a first approximation to comparability. Second, absolute increases are not directly comparable to percentage increases. The authors' absolute figures, except where negative, can neither affirm nor deny high percentage growth. Third, as a relatively minor point, county growth is not the same as city growth. Although county absolute growth in manufacturing would not ordinarily understate the comparable figure for a city within the county, it would do so where some other part of the county had experienced a loss. Fourth, manufacturing employment is not a particularly good proxy for population, and population growth is the issue. Nonmanufacturing sources of growth are overlooked, and "declines" may result from strikes or layoffs. To the extent that manufacturing affects population growth, each new manufacturing worker represents about four people—assuming an average family size of 3.33 (the 1960 national average) and an employment multiplier (new retail, service, and public employment supported by the manufacturing growth) of 1.20. Fifth, the analysis uses arbitrary standards to judge what gains are "sizable" (1,000 or more employees) or "modest" (1 to 999). To challenge the Department's contention that many cities grew rapidly, the authors show that only 30 percent of the counties involved had manufacturing employment increases of 1,000 or more. Isn't it a bit arbitrary to imply that a four-year manufacturing employment increase of, say, 700 is merely "modest"—without regard to community size?

Next, the authors argue that 1950–60 shift-share statistics show that employment growth in a majority of the "growth center" counties was due to above-average growth in nationally slow-growing industries (i.e., to shifts), not to above-average shares of nationally fast-growing industries. This supposedly refutes the Department's claim of fast growth. But the *non sequitur* is obvious. If the growth is real, the source or cause of that growth does not belie the fact that growth took place.

The authors are also wrong if they intend to imply that, because "*most of the counties on the USDA list possessed relatively slow growing* [nationally] *or declining industries*,"[4] fast growth was unlikely. This implication rests on shift-share analysis. Shift-share assumes that a place's growth rate is heavily influenced by industry mix, or its proportion of nationally fast-growing industries. The industry mix hypothesis implies that growth in most industries tends to concentrate in existing locations and proportions. Such a tendency would prevail if most growth resulted from expanded employment at existing plants and if most plants grew at their industry's national rate. But most growth is from new plants.[a] And most new plants are market-oriented. Within regions, they often locate where other plants in the same industries have not preempted local markets. Between regions, market-oriented plants gravitate to where supplies of regionally made goods are low relative to population—away from existing production in the same industry. New *branch* plants go far from the main plant so as to lower the cost (transportation) of serving regional markets. Other factors such as tight labor markets and new or declining resources also lead new plants to new places. The same factors create unequal growth rates among established plants in the same industry. Hence, it is no surprise that tests in several studies dispute the industry mix hypothesis.[5]

In their final argument, the authors view fast growth as spurious where population growth in the 1960 area was not over 5 percent and county population growth was not above the national growth rate of 13 percent. But for built-up cities with growing fringe areas, 5 percent growth in the before-annexation area might be quite consistent with overall growth of 13 or 15 percent. As for county growth rates, they can be highly misleading as proxies for city growth rates. Most counties have stable or declining rural populations. Rural decreases offset urban increases. City growth rates therefore reflect generally larger population increases divided by smaller 1960 population bases; the percentage increases are larger. Yet even with their county data, the authors can rule out less than one-sixth of the USDA cities.

The Case for Including Annexed Territory. In the absence of better evidence than supports the Berry-Lamb-Gillard position, we would have no way of knowing whether the distortion caused by annexations is generally serious. Fortunately, there is better evidence. This study, by relating population growth rates—annexations and all—to other local factors, uncovers many significant relationships. Few, if any, of these relationships are likely to be spurious. This judgment rests on (1) the large number of significant relationships found,—too large for most to have occurred by chance, (2) the extremely high significance levels reached by some of the factors, such as air service, (3) the independent findings of other research, such as plant location surveys, that many of these

---

[a]Census of manufactures figures show that U.S. manufacturing employment rose 18 percent between 1954 and 1967. The net increase in plants with twenty or more employees was also 18 percent and the gross increase (allowing for closings and relocations) obviously larger. If the new plants were almost as high as the older ones in average employment, they would thus account for the entire increase. New plants are actually smaller than average (in unknown degree), but the figures leave little doubt that new plants contributed most of the increased employment.

factors influence growth, and (4) plausible theoretical explanations—explanations that generally anticipate the findings.

If the population growth rates used in this study and by the Department were not, in general, reasonably accurate, these relationships would not have been found. Real growth would be so overshadowed by a fictitious element (annexations) that the growth rates would begin to approximate random munbers. Such quasi-random growth rates could not provide the significant relationships found. To say that the random element is present but not strong enough to hide significant relationships is to admit that the data are sufficiently accurate to be used for statistical purposes.

This does not mean that the data cannot be extremely misleading for particular cities. It is conceivable that more than one city with apparently fast growth would actually show a decline if annexed 1960 population were excluded from growth. But what might be true for individual cities cannot be true for the sample as a whole. If it were, most "fast" growth would be unreal and thus unrelated to the hypothetical causes of fast growth. Then there would be few if any significant chi-square and correlation findings.

Narrowing the Analysis

The study has two fast-slow samples, two dependent variables (not counting GRO-2:1:0, which was abandoned fairly early), and twenty-six basic independent variables—104 combinations. Each combination was analyzed for three regions (Southeast, Southwest, and overall South), each of which provided chi-square and simple, partial, and multiple correlation findings—raising the number of combinations into the thousands. Presenting the findings for all combinations would entail an overly long discussion with a great deal of duplication. Therefore, with some exceptions, only the findings for the over-10,000 sample and GRO-2:0 will be presented.

The over-10,000 sample deserves favored treatment for two reasons. First, it offers the full range of independent variables, some of which are not available with the over-5,000 sample. Second, it yielded consistently (but not invariably) higher correlations. It is thus a more sensitive instrument for detecting significant relationships. This is probably because the manufacturing element of growth has more "home town" industry—which tends not to follow conventional locational criteria—among cities below 10,000. Also, annexations and random phenomena have disproportionately heavy effects on percentage growth in the smallest cities. This leaves less for the "rational" factors being examined to explain.

GRO-2 : 0 (the fast-slow dummy) is preferred over GRO-% (percentage growth) largely because GRO-2 : 0 proved to be more sensitive. That is, it usually yielded higher correlations, indicating that it provides a better fit in measuring the relationships between growth and the independent variables. Another advantage of GRO-2 : 0—one that may help explain its greater sensitivity—is that it automatically holds constant the geographical influences that give high growth rates to cities in fast-growing states.

There is generally agreement between the over-5,000 and over-10,000 samples, as well as between GRO-% and GRO-2 : 0, as to which relationships are significant and which are the most significant. Omitting the over-5,000 and GRO-% findings therefore does not alter the thrust of the study's conclusions. Where either the over-5,000 sample or GRO-% offers findings that are exceptional or otherwise of special interest, they will be presented.

Significance Levels

In the remainder of this study, significance levels will frequently be mentioned for various chi-square and correlation findings. The 5 percent and 1 percent levels will be emphasized. The 5 percent level, of course, is the level that could be reached or exceeded by chance only 5 percent of the time, or five times in one hundred random samples; the 1 percent level could be reached by chance only 1 percent of the time.

Chi-square (χ^2), as used in this study, is computed by distributing the fast and the slow cities (two groups) among several categories defined by some other factor. The population tests, for example, distribute the cities among several population intervals, allowing the fast and slow distributions to be compared. Although most comparisons in this study start with more than three intervals, these are always combined into two or three to compute χ^2; the text tells how many. Significance depends not only on the value of χ^2 but on how many intervals are used. The 5 percent and 1 percent levels for χ^2 when the fast and slow groups are broken down into two intervals (one "degree of freedom") or three (two "degrees of freedom") are as follows:

Level	Two Intervals (1 df)	Three Intervals (2 df)
5%	3.841	5.991
1%	6.635	9.210

For simple correlations (r's), significance depends on how much r differs from .00 and on how many cases (cities) are in the sample. GRO-2 : 0 uses 58 cases in the Southeast, 58 in the Southwest, and 116 for the overall South. The 5 percent and 1 percent significance levels for r's based on these numbers of cases are as follows:

Level	Southeast	Southwest	South
5%	±.26	±.26	±.18
1%	±.34	±.34	±.24

With partial correlations (partial r's, or "partials"), one degree of freedom is lost—equivalent now to losing one case from the sample—for every variable held constant. This means that a higher r is needed to reach a given significance level. The standardized control sets (see chapter 2) hold constant twelve variables for the Southeast, fourteen for the Southwest, and fourteen for the South. The corresponding significance levels for the standardized partials are these:

Level	Southeast	Southwest	South
5%	±.29	±.30	±.20
1%	±.38	±.39	±.25

In some instances, where a variable being tested belongs to the standardized control set and is therefore not held constant, or where prior growth or unemployment is not held constant, the significance levels are .01 or .02 lower than those shown above.

Strictly speaking, these significance levels do not apply to r's based on dummy variables. The usual significance tests, used for standard tables from which the above significance levels were taken, assume a normal bivariate distribution, whereas dummy values are not normally distributed. As a practical matter, however, dummy variables usually give r's of the same general magnitude as those for the continuous variables on which they are based (when based, as here, on continuous variables). Moreover, the significance readings given above for the simple r's correspond closely to those reached with chi-square tests, which likewise are based on dichotomous (fast-slow) growth breakdowns and hold nothing constant. The conventional significance levels thus are usually good approximations to what might have been provided by a more sophisticated test if one had been available with the computer program used.[6]

Correlations for Geographic Variables

The seven geographic variables used in this study are there only for control purposes—that is, for purposes of being held constant. Their main role is to ensure that growth rate variations described by GRO-% (percentage growth) are due to local rather than regional or subregional factors. A secondary role is to provide better control over local factors held constant relative to GRO-2:0. The added control comes from controlling geographic variation in the effect of other factors (as opposed to variation in the factors themselves). But, though control is their function, one is naturally curious about their relationships to growth.

The geographic variables had the simple and (South only) standardized partial r's with GRO-% shown here:

Variable	Southeast	Southwest	South (Simple)	South (Partial)
ST-%P	+.19	+.19	+.18	+.08
ST-%M	+.19	+.05	+.09	+.19
SE-SW			−.08	−.24
COAST	−.20		−.15	−.17
DELTA		+.01	+.05	+.01
W-TEX		−.12	−.08	+.03
ISOL	−.03	−.02	+.04	+.19

These r's indicate that city population growth rates in the South tend to be (1) high in states with high population growth rates, (2) high in states with high manufacturing growth rates, (3) lower in the Southeast—where SE-SW is valued at one—than in the Southwest, (4) especially low in the five-state East Coast group, (5) about average in the three Mississippi Delta states, (6) low in sparsely developed West Texas, and (7) high in the states most isolated from the Manufacturing Belt. The Southwest's faster growth vis-à-vis the Southeast would show up better were it not for the economic stagnation of West Texas. A −.54 intercorrelation between ST-%P and W-TEX makes this point.

For GRO-%, which uses larger samples (fast-*moderate*-slow) than GRO-2 : 0, the 5 percent significance level is ±.21 for the two subregions and ±.15 (for both r and partial r) for the South. Most of the r's—all of them for the subregions—thus fall short of the 5 percent level. Yet for the South, three geographic variables reach the 1 percent level (±.19) with either their simple or their partial r.

Although these r's are not very high, it would be wrong to conclude that geography is relatively unimportant to local growth rates. The truth is obvious when one compares the 8 negative growth rates among 37 East Texas cities that survived screening with the 21 negative growth rates out of 30 in West Texas. In general, the larger and less homogeneous a region, the more important geographical influences should be. Even a region as large as the South is relatively homogeneous in the national context, whereas the United States offers extreme constrasts between the slow-growing Northeast and the fast-growing West. If all states were represented in the sample, we would expect much higher r's for geographic variables.

Intercorrelations for Independent Variables

This study is not directly concerned with the intercorrelations among the independent variables. Nevertheless, these intercorrelations provide valuable information for exploring causal relationships: they show whether two variables are related in such a way that one's relationship to growth, if significant, might result from its acting as a proxy for another. The intercorrelations also have potential value for researchers delving into other questions, such as the effect of local and subregional factors on local unemployment rates. Hence these intercorrelations merit attention.

Table 3-1 shows the intercorrelations among twenty of the more important independent variables. The findings come from the basic sample—that is, the fast-slow sample of 116 cities over 10,000 population. For simplicity, only the basic variables are listed in the row and column headings. But the intercorrelation shown for any pair of variables may actually use a derivative for one or both variables. For example, the -.33 intercorrelation between E_m/E and COL-3 is actually between the 2-1-0 dummy $E_m/E \geq 25{:}20$ and $\sqrt{COL\text{-}3}$. The table always uses that pair of variables that best measures the relationship between the two factors—the pair that maximizes the intercorrelation.

SE-SW, the Southeast-Southwest dummy, is included in the table to show how Southeast and Southwest cities differ in important respects. Since SE-SW is high (one) in the Southeast and low (zero) in the Southwest, a positive r means the intercorrelated local variable has generally higher values in the Southeast: a negative r means the opposite.

A noteworthy difference is in manufacturing. E_m/E (manufacturing employment as a percentage of total employment) has an extremely significant r of +.49 with SE-SW: southeastern cities have relatively high employment in manufacturing. VA/P (value added per capita) has an r of +.29. This verifies the Southeast's lead in manufacturing. At the same time, though, it shows that the Southeast's value added advantage is much less than its manufacturing employment advantage. Since employment (E_m/E) stresses labor-intensive industry whereas value added (VA/P) stresses capital-intensive industry, the contrasting r's amount to a finding that manufacturing is relatively labor-intensive in the Southeast—a fact well known to economists—and relatively capital-intensive in the Southwest.

EARN (wages) has an r of -.32 with SE-SW. Wages run lower in the Southeast, which explains why the Southeast attracts labor-intensive industry. This finding ties in with the r of -.26 between SE-SW and SCHOOL: southeastern cities have generally lower percentages of children in school. The lower schooling levels reflect the comparatively rural structure of southeastern society, which in turn helps explain the low wages.

The figures in Table 3-1 are for the overall South. The equivalent intercorrelations for the Southeast and Southwest are generally similar but sometimes considerably different. An extreme example is the -.14 r between E_m/E and TAX/P (property taxes per capita). The same two variables have intercorrelations of +.19 and +.31 for the Southeast and Southwest respectively—opposite in sign from the South's -.14. SE-SW explains why. E_m/E, we have already seen, runs high in the Southeast. But TAX/P runs low: its r with SE-SW is -.36. (Low wages in the Southeast result in low personal income, leading to low taxes.) The upshot is that, through Southeast-Southwest differences in manufacturing and tax levels, manufacturing and taxes are negatively intercorrelated for the overall South—even though new manufacturing generally results in higher tax revenues.

Two other intercorrelations deserve brief comment. There is a striking -.40

Table 3-1
Intercorrelations for Selected Independent Variables[a]

Variable	POP	TRADE	MFG>0	E_m/E	MFG	VA/P	AIR	HWY	COL-3
SE-SW	-.099	+.092	+.224	+.489	+.224	+.288	+.027	-.208	-.093
POP		+.715	+.482	-.130	+.341	-.029	-.574	-.018	+.319
TRADE	(Rating)		+.787	+.202	+.585	+.009	-.649	-.069	+.199
MFG>0	(Mfg. dummy)			+.371	+.831	+.176	-.518	-.155	+.087
E_m/E	(Mfg. employment %)				+.455	+.731	-.177	-.109	-.325
MFG	(R. McNally mfg. rating)					+.399	-.378	-.111	+.003
VA/P	(Value added per capita)						-.222	-.122	-.160
AIR	(Distance to commercial airport)							+.233	-.315
HWY	(Distance to Interstate highway)								-.124
COL-3	(Colleges: 3-2-1-0 = Ph.D-M.A.-B.A.-none)								
HI-SCH	(High school percentage, persons over 25)								
SCHOOL	(Percentage in school, children ages 14-17)								
D_m	(Distance to nearest metropolitan area of 250,000 or more)								
$P_m G_m$	(Population-weighted 1960-70 growth rate of D_m metropolitan area)								
EARN	(Wages: median annual earnings, operatives and kindred workers)								
TAX/P	(Property taxes per capita, county)								
RACE	(Racial mix: nonwhite population percentage)								
G:50-60	(1950-60 population growth rate)								
MIGR	(1950-60 net migration rate, county)								
UNEMP	(Unemployment rate)								

[a]Based on fast-slow sample: 116 cities over 10,000.

r between UNEMP (unemployment rate) and $P_m G_m$ (absolute growth of the nearest major metropolitan area). This supports the hypothesis that low unemployment in nonmetropolitan cities often results from job opportunities in fast-growing metropolitan areas nearby. The other *r* is that of +.39 between SCHOOL (percentage of children in school) and RACE (nonwhite population percentage). Quite contrary to expectations, this points to generally higher school attendance for blacks vis-a-vis whites. The equivalent *r*'s for the Southeast and Southwest are, respectively, +.42 and +.52; this phenomenon has nothing to do with Southeast-Southwest differences. A possible explanation is that the black population is more urbanized and thus benefits from the higher school attendance found in urban areas. If so, the connection between race and schooling supports other evidence that SCHOOL is essentially a proxy for rural-urban characteristics when it shows significant correlations with growth variables.

Notes

1. U.S. Department of Agriculture, Economic Research Service, *The Economic and Social Condition of Rural America in the 1970s* (Washington: Senate Committee on Government Operations, 1971), pp. 22-23.

2. Richard Lamb and Quentin Gillard, "Growth Center Schemes Evalu-

HI-SCH	SCHOOL	D_m	P_mG_m	EARN	TAX/P	RACE	G:50-60	MIGR	UNEMP
-.127	-.260	-.161	-.014	-.317	-.356	+.113	+.130	+.107	-.039
+.168	+.225	+.022	-.108	-.050	+.149	+.193	-.134	+.230	-.061
+.123	+.271	+.091	+.032	-.106	+.173	+.200	-.214	+.065	+.077
+.111	+.237	+.063	+.059	-.040	+.157	+.205	-.245	-.122	+.022
-.177	+.113	-.299	-.188	+.255	-.135	+.266	+.098	-.270	+.121
+.047	+.134	-.023	-.009	+.112	+.104	+.096	-.095	-.148	+.051
-.067	+.022	-.252	-.120	+.192	+.119	+.021	+.013	+.202	+.111
-.293	-.311	-.142	+.085	-.049	-.258	-.169	+.244	-.172	+.170
+.008	+.206	+.233	-.112	+.084	+.124	+.162	+.107	-.093	+.145
+.408	+.080	-.099	+.105	-.225	+.047	-.134	-.131	+.144	-.360
	+.393	+.131	+.022	+.016	+.146	-.148	+.055	+.232	-.436
		+.112	-.215	+.100	+.184	+.391	-.217	-.112	-.086
			+.290	+.137	+.229	+.062	+.066	+.018	+.100
				+.276	+.336	-.204	-.142	+.094	-.401
					+.488	-.362	-.154	+.122	-.239
						-.207	-.231	-.155	-.106
							-.204	-.150	+.314
								+.281	+.117
									-.179

ated," in Brian J.L. Berry, *Growth Centers in the American Urban System,* vol. 1 (Cambridge, Mass.: Ballinger, 1973), pp. 165–73.

3. Ibid., p. 171.

4. Ibid., p. 169.

5. See Harvey S. Perloff, Edgar S. Dunn, Jr., Eric E. Lampard, and Richard F. Muth, *Regions, Resources, and Economic Growth* (Washington: Resources for the Future, 1960), pp. 68–69; Victor R. Fuchs, *Changes in the Location of Manufacturing in the United States Since 1929* (New Haven: Yale University Press, 1962), pp. 11–12; George H. Borts and Jerome L. Stein, *Economic Growth in a Free Market* (New York: Columbia University Press, 1964), p. 46; and Robert B. Bretzfelder, "Geographic Trends in Personal Income in the 1960s," *Survey of Current Business* 50, no. 8 (August 1970): 14–23 and chart 10. Also see Leonard F. Wheat, *Regional Growth and Industrial Location: An Empirical Viewpoint* (Lexington, Mass.: D.C. Heath, 1973), p. 29.

6. An overview of the problems involved in significance testing in discriminant analysis, including that form of it that uses dummy variables, can be found in Leslie J. King, "Discriminant Analysis: A Review of Recent Theoretical Contributions and Application," *Economic Geography* 45, no. 2 (Supplement, June 1970): 367–78. Also see R.A. Fisher, "The Precision of Discriminant Functions," *Annals of Eugenics* 10 (1940): 422–29.

4

Size and Importance

The twenty-three hypotheses set forth earlier can be consolidated under ten headings: (1) size and importance, (2) manufacturing, (3) transportation, (4) education, (5) labor, (6) taxes, (7) metropolitan area proximity, (8) racial mix, (9) urban amenities, and (10) economic conditions. Variables in the first category—size and importance—test the general hypothesis that larger cities tend to grow faster because of bigger labor supplies, attractive external economies, growing manufacturing firms, and urban amenities. They also test the opposing hypothesis that small cities grow faster because of lower wages, noncompetitive labor markets, lower taxes, lower land and construction costs, and the opportunity for new firms to be dominant.

Population

Population is potentially a major influence. Yet its relationship to growth has had little attention, at least where nonmetropolitan cities of 5,000 to 50,000 are concerned.[1] For this reason, and because of continuing controversy over whether very small cities are suitable for economic development efforts, population deserves especially intensive analytical treatment. The special population-interval sample (chapter 2) was devised to provide this extra attention. Findings from this sample, which provides growth rate comparisons for cities in different population intervals, will be followed by chi-square and related findings and then by correlation tests.

Comparison of Growth Rates. The population-interval sample is designed for comparing growth rates of different-sized cities. To prevent distortion that might arise from possible links between size and geographic location, this sample gives each state the same proportion of the cities in one interval as in all the others. And, to repeat, only nonmetropolitan cities are included; so this comparison, unlike some previous ones,[2] is not influenced by the growth behavior of suburbs. The sample has 330 cities: 176 from the Southeast and 154 from the Southwest. Included are 180 in the 5,000 to 9,999 population range, 60 in the 10,000 to 14,999 range, 30 in the 15,000 to 19,999 range, 30 in the 20,000 to 29,999 range, and 30 in the 30,000 to 49,999 range.

For preliminary comparisons, the median is preferable to the mean: medians prevent distortion arising from a few extremely high growth rates. Inspection of

Table 4-1
Median Growth Rates by Population Interval

Population	Southeast		Southwest		South	
30,000 to 49,999	6.5%		9.7%		8.3%	
20,000 to 29,999	5.9%	} 5.9%	1.6%	} 3.9%	3.4%	} 5.7%
15,000 to 19,999	6.0%		8.0%		7.8%	
10,000 to 14,999	8.5%		5.9%		6.2%	
5,000 to 9,999	9.4%		6.0%		8.3%	

the medians showed that the 20,000 to 29,999 interval could be combined with the 15,000 to 19,999 interval to smooth out irregularities. Table 4-1 compares median growth rates with and without this consolidation.

When all five intervals are used, the Southeast but not the Southwest or overall South shows an apparent U-shaped relationship between population and growth: high growth at both population extremes and low growth in the middle. Combining two of the intervals, as shown, gives U-shaped growth curves to all three regions. Growth rates begin high in the highest population interval, fall to minimum levels in the 15,000 to 29,999 combined interval, and then increase in both of the remaining intervals.

If the U-shaped growth curve is more than accidental, there is a plausible explanation. Partial correlation tests with the other samples suggest that (*a*) high proportions of nonmanufacturing cities (magnets for new plants) supplement the statistical effect of a low population base on percentage growth to give high growth rates to the smallest cities while (*b*) air service and colleges help the largest. Note that fast growth among the smallest cities is chiefly a Southeast phenomenon. The Southeast is where manufacturing is relatively labor-intensive— hence labor-oriented—and often seeks the cheap, unskilled labor found in small nonmanufacturing cities. Fast growth among the largest cities occurs mainly in the Southwest. That is where industry is more capital-intensive and might prefer air service, skilled labor, or urban amenities to cheap labor.

However, the differences are statistically insignificant and probably need no explanation. Significance was tested by using mean (average) growth rates. The lowest mean for each region—always the 15,000 to 29,999 mean—was compared with the highest. A *t* test measured the significance of the differences between the high and low means. The two most significant differences could occur by chance fourteen times in one hundred experiments. These two differences were the Southeast and overall South differences between the low interval's mean and the 5,000 to 9,999 interval's mean: (1) the difference between 8.0 percent and 12.9 percent for the Southeast and (2) the difference between 7.5 and 11.3 percent for the South. The biggest difference for the Southwest was that between the low interval's mean of 6.9 and the 30,000 to 49,999 interval's mean of 15.3. This difference tested out at the 26 percent significance level. Thus, in all three regions, significance fell far short of the 5 percent level.

Table 4-2
Frequency of Cases by Population Interval

Population	Southeast		Southwest		South	
	Fast	Slow	Fast	Slow	Fast	Slow
Over-5,000 Sample						
30,000 to 49,999	3	5	5	3	8	8
20,000 to 29,999	7	8	5	10	12	18
15,000 to 19,999	4	6	5	3	9	9
10,000 to 14,999	11	17	11	12	22	29
5,000 to 9,999	45	34	34	32	79	66
Total Cities	70	70	60	60	130	130
Over-10,000 Sample						
30,000 to 49,999	5	3	6	4	11	7
20,000 to 29,999	6	6	6	10	12	16
15,000 to 19,999	4	4	6	5	10	9
10,000 to 14,999	14	16	11	10	25	26
Total Cities	29	29	29	29	58	58

Chi-Square and Related Tests. Here and elsewhere the chi-square findings are based on the fast-slow samples; the moderate-growth cities from the augmented sample are not used. (Three-column tests including the moderate cities were performed, but the findings were invariably less significant than those for fast-slow comparisons.) The findings, then, compare the population and other distributions of the fastest one-third of the nonmetropolitan cities with the distributions of the slowest one-third.

Table 4–2 looks at the population distributions of the fast and slow cities. Because of population's policy significance, and also because the over-5,000 sample provides an exceptional finding for the smallest cities, the findings for both fast-slow samples (over 5,000 and over 10,000) are covered. The only thing resembling a noteworthy fast-slow difference is the 45:34 fast-slow ratio for the smallest population interval in the over-5,000 sample's Southeast subsample. This agrees with the table 4–1 findings in suggesting that labor-oriented industry is attracted to the Southeast's smaller cities. But again the difference is not significant at the 5 percent level: χ^2 for the Southeast is only 2.90—significant at only the 10 percent level—when based on a two-interval, above-and-below-10,000 breakdown.

In the over-10,000 sample, one finds no appreciable difference between the fast and slow distributions in any region. If the two highest and two lowest intervals are combined to provide a two-interval breakdown, the South's fast distribution is identical to the slow one: both show 23 cases above 20,000 and 35 cases below.

A comparison of median populations for the fast and slow cities tells the same story. Table 4–3 shows that the fast-growing cities are (1) slightly smaller

Table 4–3
Populations Medians of Fast and Slow Cities[a]

	Southeast		Southwest		South	
Sample	Fast	Slow	Fast	Slow	Fast	Slow
Over 5,000	8,540	10,370	8,980	9,600	8,880	9,940
Over 10,000	15,310	13,850	17,420	15,950	17,190	15,500

[a]Figures are rounded.

than the slow-growing ones in the over-5,000 sample but (2) slightly larger in the over-10,000 sample. In neither sample and in none of the regional subsamples is the difference very large.

Correlation Tests. The correlation tests for population used the basic population variable, POP, and a dummy, POP $>$ 30. POP $>$ 30, suggested by the earlier findings, is valued at one where POP exceeds 30,000 and at zero elsewhere. When correlated with GRO-2:0 using the over-10,000 sample, these variables have the following simple r's:

Variable	Southeast	Southwest	South
POP	+.10	–.04	+.03
POP $>$ 30	+.10	+.09	+.10

A comparison of these r's with the 5 percent significance levels, given in chapter 3, shows that none is significant. However, as indicated by the positive r's, there is a very slight tendency for high growth to be associated with high population among cities of 10,000 to 50,000.

Turning to partial r's, we do find occasional significant partials, always negative, for POP. But these seem to result from a proxy relationship to the negative side of manufacturing: they occur when MFG $>$ 0 is not held constant, and they are lower than the corresponding partial for MFG $>$ 0. Usually, POP is not significant even when MFG $>$ 0 is not held constant. The semistandardized partials, which use the standardized control set with MFG $>$ 0 deleted, are illustrative.

Variable	Southeast	Southwest	South
POP	–.13	–.25	–.12

The standardized partials for population are quite insignificant in all regions. As said earlier, these hold constant all variables in the standardized control sets except, sometimes, G:50–60 and the UNEMP dummy, which are not controlled when they duplicate (lower the partial of) the variable being tested. The Southwest's standardized partial for POP, for example, does not hold UNEMP $\geqslant$ 4 constant. The standardized partials:

Variable	Southeast	Southwest	South
POP	−.11	−.14	−.07
POP > 30	+.01	+.21	−.04

None of these partials is close to even the 5 percent significance level. In short, when cities are alike in all important respects except population, there is no significant relationship between population and growth.

Interpretation. The findings support the conclusion that, ceteris paribus, population is not significantly related to growth rates. All tests except some partial correlation tests deny a significant relationship. The exceptional tests, which do not hold manufacturing constant, show a significantly negative relationship: low population, high growth. This appears to be a proxy relationship, with low population representing a lack of manufacturing. Evidence from this and other studies, discussed in the next chapter, suggests that new plants gravitate to non-manufacturing cities to avoid competitive labor markets.

A reservation must now be added. The special population-interval sample shows noticeably faster growth among cities of 5,000 to 10,000 in the Southeast and among cities above 30,000 in the Southwest (table 4-1). Though statistically insignificant, these findings become highly plausible in the context of subsequent findings. The next chapter (on manufacturing) highlights the relatively labor-intensive nature of manufacturing in the Southeast. Southeastern industry has a known tendency to prefer comparatively rural locations, where wages are lowest. The faster growth among the smallest cities in the Southeast seems to reflect this. The faster growth of the largest cities in the Southwest, in turn, is consistent with the idea that capital-intensive industry prefers comparatively urban locations.

Also worth comment is the contrast between POP's simple r's and its partials. The partials, even the standardized ones with manufacturing held constant, are more negatively inclined. What accounts for this? Various other partials computed before and after air service, colleges, or both were controlled indicate that the larger cities benefit more from these factors. (POP has intercorrelations for the South of −.53 with AIR > 25 and +.30 with $\sqrt{COL-3}$; only 40 percent of all sample cities but 63 percent of those within twenty-five miles of air service are above 20,000 population.) The air and college stimuli initially produce a tendency towards fast growth in the larger cities. This cancels a countervailing tendency for the smallest cities to have high percentage growth. The countervailing tendency is partly due to new plants going to formerly nonmanufacturing cities. But there is also another element in the picture. When air service, colleges, and manufacturing are all held constant, this other element prevails, causing negative partials.

What is this other element? It could be chance—random variations in growth. However, the residual tendency toward fast growth in the smaller cities probably involves a statistical factor. Because population is the rate base for computing percentage growth, there is a statistical inclination for growth to be negatively correlated with population. A fixed increase in population, whatever its cause, amounts to a larger percentage increase in a city of 10,000 than in one of 25,000. This statistical element in POP's negative r's might also contribute to the generally higher growth rates observed in nonmanufacturing cities.

General Importance

Three Rand McNally importance-rating variables, intended for evaluation of special characteristics, proved to be quite similar to POP in substance—particularly in the Southeast. The variables are BUSNS, TRADE, and MFG $>$ 0. The business rating describes the volume and variety of goods and services produced or sold, with emphasis on finance, wholesaling, retailing, and newspaper circulation; 1 describes maximum importance on a 1-2-3-4-5 scale. The trade rating describes a city's importance as a regional shopping center, with 4 describing maximum importance on a 4-3-2-1-0 scale. MFG $>$ 0 is a dummy variable based on the manufacturing importance variable MFG, which uses a 3-2-1-0 rating scale; 3 represents the highest manufacturing levels. The dummy is valued at one where MFG is 3, 2, or 1 and at zero elsewhere. The "zero" cities include (1) rated cities where manufacturing is neither the primary nor the leading secondary source of employment and (2) unrated cities. Most cities below 15,000 and many below 20,000 are unrated, while the smaller cities that *are* rated tend to be weak in the rated characteristic. Hence it is no surprise that the Rand McNally ratings are closely related to POP. For the South, BUSNS, TRADE, and MFG $>$ 0 have respective intercorrelations with POP of -.67, +.72, and +.48. (MFG, on the other hand, has only a +.34 intercorrelation with POP and often has radically different partial r's than the other three Rand McNally variables.)

Chi-Square Tests. As with POP, the chi-square tests for the above three importance variables show no significant relationships between the size-importance factor and growth. Table 4-4 summarizes the relationships for cities in the over-10,000 sample. The closest thing to a significant difference between the fast and slow cities comes from MFG $>$ 0, which in the Southwest is somewhat independent of the others. In the Southwest, MFG $>$ 0 shows a tendency for the unimportant cities to grow faster. But in this instance, χ^2 is only 3.58, a little short of the 5 percent significance level of 3.84 (for one degree of freedom). Moreover, the Southwest tendency is contradicted by that in the Southeast, where the unimportant cities are predominantly slow.

Correlation Tests. The simple r's tell almost the same story, except that one relationship is now statistically significant. A reminder: here and elsewhere, ex-

Table 4–4
Frequency of Cases by Rand McNally Rating

Rating	Southeast		Southwest		South	
	Fast	Slow	Fast	Slow	Fasr	Slow
BUSNS						
3 (important)	12	10	8	8	20	18
4 (minor)	8	6	5	8	13	14
5 (unrated)	9	13	16	13	25	26
Total Cities	29	29	29	29	58	58
TRADE						
4 & 3 (AA & A)	10	11	9	9	19	20
2 (B)	4	2	2	3	6	5
1 (C)	6	3	2	4	8	7
0 (unrated)	9	13	16	13	25	26
Total Cities	29	29	29	29	58	58
MFG > 0						
1 (important)	19	16	7	15	26	31
0 (minor or unrated)	10	13	22	14	32	27
Total Cities	29	29	29	29	58	58

cept where otherwise indicated, the reported findings are based on the over-10,000 sample with GRO-2:0 as the dependent variable. The r's, with POP included for comparison, are as follows:

Variable	Southeast	Southwest	South
POP	+.10	−.04	+.03
BUSNS	−.12	+.06	−.03
TRADE	+.04	−.05	−.01
MFG > 0	+.11	−.28	−.09

Because BUSNS is low in the large cities and high in the small ones, negative for it is generally equivalent to positive for the others, and vice versa. (When r is close to zero, however, the signs may not be opposite.)

The r of −.28 for MFG > 0 in the Southwest describes the one significant relationship. Here significance reaches the 5 percent level. Since only MFG > 0 is significant, it seems that whatever causes the tendency for unimportant cities to grow faster is more closely related to manufacturing than to population, business activity, or trade. It also seems that this factor is significant only in the Southwest.

But partial r's raise other possibilities. By using the standardized control sets (chapter 2), but with MFG > 0 deleted, one can get significant r's for all regions. In the Southeast, TRADE is as high as MFG > 0. The following partials, which do not control MFG > 0, will be considered the standardized ones not only for MFG > 0 but for BUSNS and TRADE as well:

Variable	Southeast	Southwest	South
POP	−.13	−.25	−.12
BUSNS	+.30	+.36	+.14
TRADE	−.39	−.36	−.17
MFG > 0	−.39	−.45	−.27

In the Southeast, TRADE and MFG > 0 are significant at the 1 percent level, BUSNS at the 5 percent level. In the Southwest, only MFG > 0 reaches the 1 percent level, but BUSNS and TRADE are close at about the 2 percent level. Only MFG > 0 is significant for the overall South; it reaches the 1 percent level again.

When MFG > 0 is returned to the control sets (i.e., is held constant in addition to the other standardized control variables), we get these nonstandardized partials for BUSNS and TRADE, again shown in comparison with POP:

Variable	Southeast	Southwest	South
POP	−.11	−.14	−.07
BUSNS	+.09	+.16	+.05
TRADE	−.17	−.13	−.04

To repeat, the plus sign with BUSNS is equivalent to minus with POP and TRADE, because BUSNS gives its lowest values to the most important cities. All of the above partials are well short of significance. This suggests that BUSNS and TRADE, when significant under different controls, serve mainly as proxies for MFG > 0.

However, they might have a substantial degree of independent significance in the Southeast. Under most control combinations, TRADE's partial is higher than MFG > 0's in the Southeast; sometimes BUSNS also outscores MFG > 0 and even TRADE. And the Southeast's best eleven-variable multiple correlation set (chapter 14, table 14–2) includes both TRADE and MFG > 0, with TRADE as the more significant. If all variables but TRADE and MFG > 0 from that set are held constant, the partials are -.54 for TRADE and -.52 for MFG > 0. TRADE remains significant at -.34 if MFG > 0 is then controlled (ten variables held constant); BUSNS reads +.29.

Interpretation. Is business and trade importance significant in its own right? Or is it essentially a proxy for manufacturing importance? MFG > 0's Southwest partial is far above the others, allowing scant doubt as to who is a proxy for whom there. Clearly, and notwithstanding the possibility that the statistical element in POP has some effect on MFG > 0, it is MFG > 0 that dominates in the Southwest. And—this point is expanded in the next chapter—southwestern manufacturing has characteristics that do *not* call for the cheap, unskilled labor supplies that often attract southeastern plants to small, unimportant places.

The Southeast, on the other hand, has TRADE performing on par with MFG > 0. This does not necessarily contradict the idea that lack of manufacturing is behind the significant partials for TRADE and BUSNS. TRADE's performance could result from its higher Southeast intercorrelation with POP (+.67 compared with +.49 for MFG > 0): TRADE might secondarily describe the statistical effect of low population on percentage growth, while TRADE's +.85 intercorrelation with MFG > 0 would allow it to primarily identify nonmanufacturing cities.

Yet it is also possible that TRADE, BUSNS, and MFG > 0 represent a more general phenomenon, of which they emphasize different facets. This phenomenon would be the locational pull of noncompetitive labor markets on labor-intensive industry. Since labor-intensive industry is common in the Southeast but not in the Southwest, it is logical enough that TRADE and BUSNS would be significant only in the Southeast. Labor market competition can drive wages up when new manufacturing enters a city where business is already important; at any rate, this is known to happen where the established business is manufacturing. Perhaps MFG > 0 emphasizes the manufacturing facet of the labor market, while BUSNS and TRADE (which have a −.91 intercorrelation) stress commercial hiring. If so, BUSNS and TRADE are partly proxies for MFG > 0 but partly significant in their own right.

To be sure, TRADE's strong showing in the Southeast could result from spurious correlation, enhanced by a strong intercorrelation with MFG > 0. But other variables, especially those measuring schooling, wages, taxes, and metropolitan area proximity, describe similar Southeast-Southwest contrasts. Growth in the Southeast favors comparatively rural—small, unimportant, remote—cities where labor conditions are attractive to labor-intensive manufacturing. Trade, like manufacturing, contributes to urbanization and could well preempt important shares of local labor supplies. TRADE and BUSNS therefore probably have a genuine degree of independent significance—which is what the previously mentioned multiple correlation combination seems to indicate.

Notes

1. Most studies comparing population and growth have limited relevance for present purposes. Some focus on metropolitan areas; some focus on small towns below 2,500 or at least give such towns great weight in their analyses; some fail to differentiate between suburbs and nonmetropolitan cities; some use county data in lieu of city data. One study that *is* relevant deserves mention. This is Glenn V. Fuguitt, "The Places Left Behind: Population Trends and Policy for Rural America," *Rural Sociology* 36, no. 4 (December 1971): 449–67. Fuguitt

looks at 1950–60 and 1960–70 population growth for U.S. cities. He finds almost identical growth rate distributions for nonmetropolitan cities in two size categories: 2,500 to 9,999 and 10,000 or more. Although a more detailed size breakdown would strengthen the findings, they suggest no connection between size and growth for cities above 2,500. However, growth rates do show a progressive decline over three successively lower population intervals below 2,500.

2. See, for example, Ray M. Northam, "Population Size, Relative Location, and Declining Urban Centers: Conterminous United States, 1940–1960," *Land Economics* 45, no. 3 (August 1969): 315.

5 Manufacturing

In theory, already established manufacturing might help or hinder a city's growth. It would help if the established firms were growing rapidly, if they attracted supplier or consumer industries, or if they created external economies (e.g., skilled labor, freight forwarding) that attracted new plants. Manufacturing would hinder growth if the established firms were stagnating or declining, if they were viewed by location-seeking firms as sources of recruitment and wage competition, if they had histories of labor trouble, if they opposed local promotion designed to attract new manufacturing to the labor market, or if potential new firms wanted community influence.

Findings for Manufacturing

The study uses three basic manufacturing variables: MFG (Rand McNally manufacturing rating), VA/P (manufacturing value added per capita), and E_m/E (manufacturing employment as a percentage of total employment). VA/P and E_m/E differ insofar as the employment measure emphasizes labor-intensive industry while the value measure emphasizes capital-intensive industry. Still, VA/P and E_m/E are closely related, having an intercorrelation of +.73 for the South. MFG is more independent, showing intercorrelations of only +.40 with VA/P and +.44 with E_m/E. This relative independence reflects the lack of MFG ratings for many small cities, which are treated as though they have no manufacturing even when they do. MFG nevertheless tends to imitate VA/P in its partial correlation behavior. Also, MFG is closer to VA/P than to E_m/E in its intercorrelation with SE-SW (Southeast-Southwest dummy): their intercorrelations are +.22 for MFG, +.29 for VA/P, and +.49 for E_m/E, with MFG and VA/P both seeming to describe the relatively small Southeast-Southwest differences in capital-intensive manufacturing. MFG, then, can be viewed as primarily measuring capital-intensive industry.

Chi-Square Tests. Table 5-1 is the basis for manufacturing's chi-square tests. VA (total value added) replaces VA/P in the table, because VA/P was generated by computer in the correlation program and was not available for chi-square purposes. VA is partly a proxy for POP and therefore might easily be misinterpreted. But any strongly positive or negative relationship between VA and growth could not be due to population, for POP is not significantly related to growth.

37

Table 5-1
Frequency of Cases by Extent of Manufacturing

	Southeast		Southwest		South	
Manufacturing Level	Fast	Slow	Fast	Slow	Fast	Slow
MFG[a]						
3 (Mm)	6	5	2	3	8	8
2 (Mx)	5	3	2	3	7	6
1 (Xm)	8	8	3	9	11	17
0 (Xx or unrated)	10	13	22	14	32	27
Total Cities	29	29	29	29	58	58
VA (millions)						
$30 or more	5	1	1	2	6	3
$10 to $29	8	16	8	10	16	26
$5 to $9	11	8	1	7	12	15
$0 to $4	5	4	19	10	24	14
Total Cities	29	29	29	29	58	58
E_m/E						
36% or more	6	10	1	1	7	11
26% to 35%	4	7	3	4	7	11
21% to 25%	5	6	3	5	8	11
16% to 20%	8	6	3	5	11	11
11% to 15%	4	0	5	5	9	5
6% to 10%	1	0	10	6	11	6
0% to 5%	1	0	4	3	5	3
Total Cities	29	29	29	29	58	58

[a]In the parenthetical ratings under MFG, upper and lower case letters respectively identify the primary and leading secondary economic activity. M stands for manufacturing, and X stands for any other economic activity.

The table shows a general tendency, subject to exceptions, toward fast growth in the least industrialized cities—which is consistent with the earlier finding for MFG > 0. This tendency is strongest for MFG and VA in the Southwest and for E_m/E in the Southeast. For MFG, the Southwest χ^2 of 3.58, based on two intervals (zero and above-zero), was seen before with MFG > 0 and is not quite significant. But for VA, the Southwest's 19 to 10 majority in favor of "fast" among cities with value added of less than $5 million is significant: χ^2 is 4.41, exceeding the 5 percent level, when a two-way breakdown is used for VA (three highest intervals combined into one). VA's χ^2 for the overall South is 4.26, again significant at the 5 percent level.

Neither MFG nor VA shows any tendency for growth to decrease as manufacturing levels increase above the lowest interval. This suggests that the relationship these variables detect stems from the presence or absence (or near absence) of manufacturing rather than from the amount.

In the Southeast, and to a lesser extent in the Southwest, E_m/E also points to faster growth among nonmanufacturing cities. When the Southeast cases are regrouped as shown, χ^2 is 3.95, significant at the 5 percent level.

Interval	Fast	Slow
20% and up	16	24
0 to 19%	13	5

E_m/E's χ^2 is also significant for the overall South when cities are classified according to whether their table 5-1 intervals are higher than, the same as, or lower than the interval containing the subregional (Southeast or Southwest) median for E_m/E. This breakdown compensates for the generally lower manufacturing levels found in the Southwest.

Interval	Fast	Slow
Above median E_m/E	20	32
At median E_m/E	10	11
Below median E_m/E	28	15

Both this breakdown and the original breakdown for the Southeast show a tendency for growth to decline as E_m/E increases. This might indicate that E_m/E measures a somewhat different facet of manufacturing than MFG and VA. Since E_m/E emphasizes labor-intensive industry whereas VA emphasizes capital-intensive industry, this different facet could be well-known tendency toward slow growth in labor-intensive industries. More will be said about this tendency later.

Despite this evidence of faster growth in nonmanufacturing cities, MFG and VA provide some contradictory evidence for the Southeast. For manufacturing cities (rated above zero), MFG shows a slight inclination for growth to increase with increases in manufacturing; a U-shaped curve with fast growth at both manufacturing extremes is suggested. VA, in turn, shows a very interesting 5:1 fast-slow ratio for cities with value added of $30 million and up. Though not statistically significant (too few cases), this 5:1 ratio, taken in conjunction with the earlier findings for E_m/E, suggests a new hypothesis: cities where capital-intensive manufacturing (VA) is high tend to grow fast, but cities where labor-intensive manufacturing (E_m/E) is high tend to grow slowly.

Correlation Tests. The correlation tests for manufacturing use ten variables: MFG, MFG > 0, VA/P, VA $\geqslant 5$, E_m/E, and five dummies based on E_m/E. The variables with symbols are dummies valued at one where the indicated value is exceeded ($>$) or else equaled or exceeded ($\geqslant$) by the basic variable and at zero elsewhere. The best E_m/E dummy is $E_m/E \geqslant 25{:}20{:}15$, a 3-2-1-0 dummy valued at three where E_m/E reaches 25 percent, at two for 20 to 24 percent, and so on. Each variable gives its highest value to the cities with the most manufacturing, so positive r's mean that manufacturing cities grow fast and negative r's mean the opposite. To repeat, all r's in this study, unless otherwise indicated, come from the over-10,000 sample and use GRO-2:0 as the dependent variable. We begin with manufacturing's simple r's:

Variable	Southeast	Southwest	South
MFG	+.11	−.20	−.03
MFG > 0	+.11	−.28	−.09
VA/P	+.01	−.07	−.03
VA ⩾ 5	−.05	−.28	−.17
E_m/E	−.24	−.16	−.18
E_m/E ⩾ 25:20:15	−.33	−.15	−.21

Three tendencies seen with chi-square are again evident. First is a tendency, very faint as yet, toward faster growth in Southeast cities with high manufacturing levels. MFG and VA/P reveal this. Second is an opposing tendency for growth to decline as the manufacturing *employment* percentage goes up, particularly in the Southeast. E_m/E ⩾ 25:20:15's reading of −.33, significant at almost the 1 percent level (±.34), brings this out. Third, there is a related tendency toward high growth rates in cities with extremely low manufacturing levels. This is clearest in the Southwest, where MFG > 0 and VA ⩾ 5 both have r's of −.28, significant at the 5 percent level.

Partial r's sharpen our view of these tendencies. The standardized control sets (chapter 2) include MFG > 0 and, except in the Southwest, MFG. (MFG largely duplicates MFG > 0 in the Southwest.) If these variables are deleted from the control sets and the remaining variables are held constant, the partials shown below result:

Variable	Southeast	Southwest	South
MFG	+.03	−.39	−.07
MFG > 0	−.23	−.45	−.23
VA/P	+.21	−.03	+.09
VA ⩾ 5	−.21	−.45	−.27
E_m/E	−.16	−.23	−.11
E_m/E ⩾ 25:20:15	−.22	−.27	−.14

Several changes are apparent. First, one of the positive variables, VA/P, has gone from +.01 to +.21 in the Southeast, approaching significance. The other positive variable, MFG, has diverged from MFG > 0 by .26, whereas their simple r's are identical. Second, MFG > 0 and VA ⩾ 5 are now much more negative— mainly because controlling colleges and air service has eliminated two advantages of large cities, where the manufacturing dummies are usually high (valued at one instead of zero). Both dummies are significant at the 1 percent level in the Southwest; VA ⩾ 5 reaches the 1 percent level for the South. Third, E_m/E ⩾ 25:20:15 is now insignificant in the Southeast. This is because it cannot reflect colleges now that COL-3 is held constant.

Restoring the negative manufacturing variable—MFG > 0—to the standardized control sets provides the standardized partials for the positive variables, MFG and VA/P; it also provides useful nonstandardized partials for $E_m/E \geqslant$ 25:20:15. The partials:

Variable	Southeast	Southwest	South
MFG	+.34	+.08	+.18
VA/P	+.20	+.05	+.08
$E_m/E \geqslant 25:20:15$	−.26	−.11	−.14

Released from the negative pull of nonmanufacturing cities, which pull is controlled by MFG > 0, MFG has climbed well above the 5 percent level in the Southeast and is only a point short for the South. But $E_m/E \geqslant 25:20:15$ is still negative, though no longer significant. Its strength is mainly in the Southeast; controlling MFG > 0 drives $E_m/E \geqslant 25:20:15$ down from −.27 to −.11 in the Southwest. Indications are that in the Southeast, but not the Southwest, growth decreases as manufacturing employment increases within the manufacturing subset of cities.

The residual tendency toward slow growth in cities with high manufacturing employment percentages obscures the full magnitude of manufacturing's positive side. But if $E_m/E \geqslant 25:20:15$ is now added to the other variables held constant, these partials result:

Variable	Southeast	Southwest	South
MFG	+.48	+.04	+.26
VA/P	+.33	+.07	+.20

MFG's partials are now significant at the 1 percent level for Southeast and the overall South. VA/P reaches the 5 percent level in these regions. Manufacturing indeed seems to have a positive side—something that leads to high growth in cities with high manufacturing value added.

What happens if this positive side, best represented by MFG, is held constant in the Southeast and South? (MFG duplicates the negative variables in the Southwest and, held constant, lowers their r's). Restoring MFG to the standardized control sets and dropping MFG > 0 provides the standardized partials for the negative variables. For the Southeast, some nonstandardized partials with MFG > 0 also held constant ("MFG > 0 In"—in the control set) are also shown. These extra partials demonstrate the presence of *two* negative facets of manufacturing, the MFG > 0 facet and the E_m/E facet. The partials:

Variable	Southeast		Southwest	South
	MFG > 0 Out	MFG > 0 In		
MFG > 0	−.39		−.45	−.27
VA $\geqslant$ 5	−.21	−.27	−.45	−.26
$E_m/E \geqslant 25:20:15$	−.22	−.43	−.27	−.14
VA/P	+.21	+.05	−.03	+.11

The first thing to note is that MFG > 0, describing cities with little or no manufacturing (where the dummy is valued at zero), is now highly significant: it exceeds the 1 percent level in all three regions. A similar variable, VA $\geqslant 5$, does just as well in the Southwest and South. Next, as a surprise, $E_m/E \geqslant 25{:}20{:}15$ is not only more significant when MFG > 0 is held constant in the Southeast but actually climbs well above the 1 percent level. This shows that MFG > 0 and E_m/E ultimately describe different forces; otherwise holding MFG > 0 constant would lower the E_m/E partial. Finally, and as added evidence of manufacturing's positive side, VA/P remains positive even though its positive companion, MFG, is controlled.

Interpretation of Findings

The findings show that some manufacturing variables are positive and others are negative. MFG and VA/P are generally positive, becoming significantly so when MFG > 0—or else a combination of MFG > 0 and $E_m/E \geqslant 25{:}20{:}15$—is held constant. MFG > 0 and VA $\geqslant 5$ are generally negative, becoming significantly negative when MFG is held constant. E_m/E is also generally negative and becomes significantly negative in the Southeast when MFG and MFG > 0 are controlled. This means that E_m/E, though it initially involves some duplication of MFG > 0 and VA $\geqslant 5$, has important substantive differences from the other negative variables. We thus have evidence of three tendencies—one positive and two negative. What accounts for this?

Capital-Intensive Industry. One clue is the contrast between VA/P, measuring value added and showing positive r's, and E_m/E, measuring manufacturing employment and showing negative r's. To repeat, value added emphasizes capital-intensive industry, where high capital-to-labor ratios explain the high value added. Employment emphasizes labor-intensive industry, which can have high employment without high value added. It may be, then, that capital-intensive industry (positive) involves one growth tendency and labor-intensive industry (negative) another.

A tendency toward slow growth in labor-intensive industries has already been mentioned, and this entails a corollary tendency toward fast growth in capital-intensive industries. The five most labor-intensive manufacturing industries, as measured by 1954 wages as a percentage of value added, are textiles, leather and leather goods, lumber and wood products, apparel, and furniture and fixtures—in that order.[1] These five industries rank near the bottom and in reverse order—19th, 18th, 17th, 14th, and 13th, respectively—when all twenty two-digit manufacturing industries are ranked by 1939–54 manufacturing employment growth rate.[2] Thus, one recent study can point out that "in the current U.S. economy, the growth industries . . . have tended to be industries with relatively high capital-labor ratios."[3]

Very likely, the positive side of manufacturing—MFG and VA/P—relates to the growth of established industry in cities with fast-growing, capital-intensive manufacturing. It could also represent the availability of skilled labor (associated with capital-intensive industry) and other external economies in cities with high capital-intensive manufacturing levels.

This does not explain why capital-intensive industry lacks significantly positive r's in the Southwest. Part of the answer lies in duplication of MFG by metropolitan area proximity variables, included in the Southwest's standardized control set. If $D_m > 160$ (a distance-to-nearest-"metro" dummy) and $P_m G_m$ ("metro" population weighted by growth) are dropped from the control set, MFG's partial is +.23 instead of +.08. Beyond this, the relative lack of manufacturing in the Southwest probably makes the manufacturing simulus less important.

Labor-Intensive Industry. E_m/E, in turn, would seem to describe the generally slow growth in cities with labor-intensive industry. To the extent that this slow growth is independent of the related tendency for nonmanufacturing cities to grow fast, it probably comes mostly from slow growth in the industries themselves. It could also result, at least partly, from progressively higher wage levels in cities with progressively higher levels of labor-intensive manufacturing: there is a +.50 intercorrelation between EARN (wages) and E_m/E in the Southeast. Although EARN (median annual earnings, operatives) is in the standardized control set, it is a crude measure of wages and should not completely control the wage influence.

The idea that E_m/E's significance derives from labor-oriented industry is supported by the importance of such industry in the South. After World War II, and particularly in the 1950s, the South attracted many labor-oriented plants. Textiles, the country's most labor-intensive industry, led the way. Southern industrialization gained considerable impetus from a shift of textiles from New England and the Middle Atlantic states to the Southeast. The influx centered in the Carolinas, where textiles accounted for 54 percent of all manufacturing employment in 1954; the Georgia figure was 34 percent.[4] Other industry, much of it labor-oriented, followed.

The big attraction for textiles and other labor-oriented industries was abundant, cheap labor. For this reason, many of the plants went to small cities and towns, where wages were lowest. Lonsdale and Browning can thus observe that "the lack of a big-city orientation is one of the most fundamental characteristics of Southern manufacturing."[5] Again: "The very character of Southern manufacturing—labor intensive, low profit margin, with the achievement of labor economies often essential to maintain a competitive market position—tends to discourage many manufacturers from 'concentrating' in larger cities."[6] High wages and tight labor markets offset certain obvious advantages of urban locations. Thus, in the 1960s, three-fifths of the South's new in-city plants went to cities below 25,000 population[7]—powerful evidence of southern manufacturing's orientation toward cheap labor. And, switching to employment as the measure of manufacturing, one finds that the nonmetropolitan counties of the South gained more manufacturing jobs between 1960 and 1970 than the metropolitan counties.[8]

E_m/E's greater significance in the Southeast agrees with the labor interpretation of E_m/E. Within the South, labor-oriented industry has favored the Southeast over the Southwest. Let us again look at the textile industry—the largest of the labor-oriented industries. The five states with the largest relative increases in textile employment between 1939 and 1954 were North Carolina, South Carolina, Georgia, Alabama, and Virginia.[9] In 1967 the Southeast, as defined in this study (eight states), had 72 percent of the nation's textile employment.[10] Labor-oriented firms prefer the Southeast because wages are generally lower there than in the Southwest. Also, outside of Mississippi, rural population density is often too low in the Southwest to give rural cities adequate supplies of cheap labor; whereas in the Southeast, according to Lonsdale and Browning, more plants can draw on heavily rural labor markets by exploiting rural labor's willingness to accept long-distance commuting to factories.[11]

The relatively labor-intensive character of industry in the Southeast vis-à-vis the Southwest is crucial in explaining many Southeast-Southwest differences that will be encountered—in addition to the difference just observed for E_m/E. Therefore, before proceeding further, we will do well to review other evidence establishing that the Southeast's industry actually *is* more labor-intensive. First, let us recall the correlations presented for geographic variables in chapter 3. SE-SW (the 1–0 Southeast-Southwest dummy) has an *r* of +.49 with E_m/E but of only +.29 with VA/P. This shows that the Southeast has a greater advantage over the Southwest in manufacturing employment than it has in value added. The clear implication is that the Southeast has a higher ratio of labor to capital.

Next, we can look at VA/E_m—value added per manufacturing employee— which is a basic measure of labor-intensiveness: industries with relatively low VA/E_m are labor-intensive. By relating total manufacturing value added (VA) to total manufacturing employment (E_m), as reported in the *1967 Census of Manufactures* for the states in question, we get these values:

Variable	Southeast	Southwest	All Other Regions
VA/E_m	$11,666	$14,675	$13,832

Note that the Southwest, supported by oil-related industries in Louisiana ($16,962) and Texas ($16,611), is actually more capital-intensive than the rest of the nation by this measure.

Finally, we can look at employment in the previously named five most labor-intensive industries as a percentage of total manufacturing employment. Again using employment totals from the *1967 Census of Manufactures*, we get these percentages (the textile industry is shown separately because of its importance):

Industries	Southeast	Southwest	All Other Regions
Textiles	21%	2%	2%
All five	44%	20%	14%

The Southeast has more than double the Southwest's proportion of labor-intensive industry. It might be added that the Carolinas and Georgia, which provide 30 of the 58 Southeast cities in the over-10,000 sample, give the five industries 60 percent of their combined manufacturing employment.

Nonmanufacturing Cities. The negative side of manufacturing has a second facet not covered by E_m/E. This facet appeared first in MFG > 0's almost significant χ^2 of 3.58 and in significant simple r's of -.28 for both MFG > 0 and VA $\geqslant 5$ in the Southwest—the subregion where E_m/E is not significant. It was seen again in standardized partials of -.39 for MFG > 0 in the Southeast and -.45 for both MFG > 0 and VA $\geqslant 5$ in the Southwest—partials running much higher than corresponding ones for E_m/E. Unlike E_m/E and the dummies based on it, MFG > 0 and VA $\geqslant 5$ identify (value at zero) cities with ultralow manufacturing levels. The negative r's signify high growth in these nonmanufacturing cities.

The most plausible explanation for this is related to, but not the same as, the wage explanation given earlier as a possible reason for E_m/E's negative r's. Nonmanufacturing cities are probably sought primarily to avoid labor market competition—wage and hiring competition. Partly, this is still a matter of seeking low wages. But equally, it is a matter of avoiding those low-wage communities where wages would soon be forced up by the entry of another manufacturing firm in a one-industry town. A nonmanufacturing city likewise affords protection against future labor market competition. In reporting the findings of their interview survey of southern manufacturing, McLaughlin and Robock state: "One way in which a number of companies in the shoe, textile, and apparel groups thought they could safeguard their labor supply was by locating in a small town. If the new plant provided employment for most of the available labor, it was felt that other factories would not be likely to move in and compete for the labor."[12]

Access to the best workers and community influence are other reasons for locating in nonmanufacturing cities. Another McLaughlin and Robock finding is that "the preference for a small community was always qualified to exclude any town already dominated by an existing plant because . . . the company felt if its plant was relatively small that it would be likely to get the dregs of the labor market and also because such cities are 'often controlled politically or otherwise by the dominating industry.'"[13]

For related reasons, existing firms may discourage promotion designed to attract more industry. One finding of a case study of Hopkinsville, Kentucky, was that the Chamber of Commerce and other promotional groups were influenced by established manufacturing firms. "These firms were concerned about the possible competition for labor that would be engendered by newly-arriving industries. As a result, they discouraged, whenever possible, prospective firms interested in the area."[14]

The idea that nonmanufacturing cities are sought suggests a U-shaped curve relating MFG to growth. MFG is a 3–2–1–0 variable, where 3 designates cities in which manufacturing is both the primary and the leading secondary economic activity. MFG is positive and significant when MFG > 0 (or TRADE) is held constant, and this indicates that cities with 3 and 2 ratings tend to grow fast. Yet MFG > 0 is significantly negative when MFG is controlled, indicating fast growth in the 0-rating category. This U-shaped curve will be used later in formulas for predicting growth.

Colleges. One other explanation for manufacturing's relationship to growth demands attention. This explanation applies to E_m/E's good showing in the chi-square and simple correlation tests but not to the partial correlation findings. A low manufacturing employment percentage often reflects the presence of a college—the real reason for growth. College-related employment in college towns preempts a large share of the employment percentage pie, leaving less for manufacturing.

Seven of nine college towns in the Southeast have E_m/E values below 20 percent; all seven are fast-growing. Twelve of thirteen college towns in the Southwest are below 20 percent for E_m/E; ten are fast-growing. Similarly, the Southeast shows an intercorrelation of -.44 between $E_m/E \geq 25{:}15$ and $\sqrt{COL\text{-}3}$; low E_m/E goes with high college ratings. A comparable intercorrelation for the Southwest is only -.21. This helps explain why E_m/E is significant by chi-square and simple correlation tests in the Southeast but not the Southwest.

A chi-square retest of E_m/E for the Southeast confirms that the earlier finding of significance depended heavily on the college influence. Two comparisons of E_m/E and percentage growth are shown. The first, shown previously, includes all southeastern cities; the second is limited to noncollege cities.

	All Cities		Noncollege Cities	
Interval	Fast	Slow	Fast	Slow
20% and up	16	24	15	23
0 to 19%	13	5	6	5

For all cities, χ^2 is 3.95, significant at the 5 percent level. But for the noncollege cities, χ^2 is 1.64, very insignificant.

This does not mean that E_m/E has no independent significance. We saw earlier that $E_m/E \geq 25{:}20{:}15$ reaches a partial r of -.43 when all the variables in the Southeast's standardized control set—including COL-3, MFG, and MFG > 0—are held constant. This highly significant partial clearly does not hinge on a college proxy relationship. Despite initial support from colleges, E_m/E ultimately has independent significance.

Notes

1. Victor R. Fuchs, *Changes in the Location of Manufacturing in the United States Since 1929* (New Haven: Yale University Press, 1962), p. 166, table 6:10.

2. Harvey S. Perloff, Edgar S. Dunn, Jr., Eric E. Lampard, and Richard F. Muth, *Regions, Resources, and Economic Growth* (Washington, D.C.: Resources for the Future, 1960), p. 391.

3. Abt Associates, Inc., *The Industrialization of Southern Rural Areas* (Washington, D.C.: Economic Development Administration, Contract No. 7-35482, 1968), p. 5.

4. Percentages computed from U.S. Bureau of the Census, *1954 Census of Manufactures,* vol. 3, state reports, table 5.

5. Richard E. Lonsdale and Clyde E. Browning, "Rural-Urban Locational Preferences of Southern Manufacturers," *Annals of the Association of American Geographers* 61 (June 1971): 260.

6. Ibid.

7. Ibid., p. 262. Lonsdale and Browning exclude Kentucky, Oklahoma, and Texas from their definition of the South; otherwise, the states are the same as those used in the present study.

8. Niles M. Hansen, *The Future of Nonmetropolitan America* (Lexington, Mass.: D.C. Heath and Co., 1973), p. 14.

9. Perloff et al., *Regions,* p. 417. Cf. Fuchs, *Manufacturing,* p. 23.

10. Computed from U.S. Bureau of the Census, *1967 Census of Manufactures,* vol. 2, pt. 1, pp. 22-23.

11. Lonsdale and Browning, "Rural-Urban Preferences," p. 261.

12. Glenn E. McLaughlin and Stefan Robock, *Why Industry Moves South* (Washington, D.C.: National Planning Association, 1949), p. 69.

13. Ibid., p. 101; cf. p. 99.

14. Arthur D. Little, Inc., *Economic Transition of Distressed Communities* (prepared for Economic Development Administration, U.S. Department of Commerce, Contract No. 2-36725) (Cambridge, Mass.: 1974), vol. 1, p. III-1. Also see p. II-41.

6 Transportation

Because it is potentially a magnet for industry, good transportation is hypothetically related to fast growth. Air service may attract new plants—branch plants especially—by providing fast, convenient passenger connections with industrial consumers, suppliers, and company headquarters. Interstate System highways may attract plants by providing lower shipping costs and better service. Waterways (barge service) could attract firms that receive raw materials by water or, less commonly, that ship finished goods by water. Rail service, though more widely available, might sometimes affect the choice of a community; but a good statistical criterion for measuring rail service is lacking. The tests in this chapter will therefore cover air, highway, and waterway variables but not rail variables.

Air Service

Other research points to a significant relationship between a city's growth and its distance from the nearest commercial airport.[1] The basic air service variable is therefore AIR, distance in road miles from city center to the nearest airport with commercial airline service. (Airline route maps were used to identify cities with air service; road maps gave the approximate locations of airports, with 5 miles being used as a minimum distance to avoid false precision in differentiating among cities with close-in airports.) Other air service variables, derived from AIR, will be described later.

Chi-Square Tests. Table 6–1 compares the distance-to-airport distributions for the fast and slow cities. As in the earlier chi-square analysis for population, findings for the over-5,000 sample are included along with the regular over-10,000 findings. The over-5,000 sample is of interest for its evidence that cities located 40 to 50 miles from an airport may derive at least limited benefits from the related air service.

The over-5,000 sample shows a clear tendency for the cities with the closest air service to grow faster, particularly in the Southeast. Except among southwestern cities more than 50 miles from air service, all three regions show that with each increase in distance the proportion of cities that are fast-growing decreases. The Southeast shows a very sharp drop in the proportion of fast-growing cities for distances above 50 miles; cities located 41 to 50 miles from air service have generally faster growth than those located beyond 50 miles. When the

Table 6–1
Frequency of Cases by Distance to Airport

Distance	Southeast		Southwest		South	
	Fast	*Slow*	*Fast*	*Slow*	*Fast*	*Slow*
Over-5,000 Sample						
51 miles or more	9	25	23	20	32	45
41 to 50 miles	13	13				
36 to 50 miles			7	16	25	33
31 to 40 miles	11	9				
26 to 35 miles			12	12	25	20
5 to 30 miles	37	23				
5 to 25 miles	—	—	18	12	48	32
Total Cities	70	70	60	60	130	130
Over-10,000 Sample						
41 miles or more	5	16	8	12	13	28
31 to 40 miles	4	4				
26 to 40 miles			5	6	11	10
5 to 30 miles	20	9				
5 to 25 miles	—	—	16	11	34	20
Total Cities	29	29	29	29	58	58

Southeast's two middle intervals are combined to provide a three-way breakdown, χ^2 is 10.86. This is significant at the 1 percent level. The Southwest differences are not significant, because (as we shall soon see) the cities without air service have a compensatory advantage in nonmanufacturing status. The overall South has differences significant at about the 1.5 percent level: χ^2 is 6.16, when based on the three-interval breakdown used with the Southeast.

In the over-10,000 sample, both subregions indicate that most cities over 40 miles from air service are slow-growing. Most cities within 25 or 30 miles are fast-growing. Those at intermediate distances are about equally likely to be fast or slow. When the two intervals below 40 miles are combined into one, providing a two-way breakdown, the fast-slow differences are significant at the 1 percent level for the Southeast ($\chi^2 = 7.46$) and the South ($\chi^2 = 7.39$).

In neither sample do cities located very close to airports—within 10 or 15 miles—show an extra advantage when compared to cities at slightly greater distances. This suggests that cities served by an airport located in a nearby city may be about as attractive as those with their own airports; a driving time not over roughly a half hour seems more decisive than actually having an airport. However, other research has indicated a linear relationship between growth and distance, with cities that have close-in airports doing best.[2] Either way, successive increases in distance beyond 25 or 30 miles seem to bring increasingly lower growth potential.

Correlation Tests. AIR and many variables based on it were used in the correlation tests. Some of the derived variables used functional relationships, such as AIR^2, logAIR, 1/AIR, and a probability function with a growth-distance relationship described by one side of a bell-shaped curve. But the most effective variables were dummies. In the Southeast, the 1-0 dummy AIR > 30 and the 2-1-0 dummy AIR > 40:30 did best; in the Southwest and South, AIR > 25 and AIR > 40:25 were strongest. Since AIR and the dummies are lowest (i.e., distance is lowest) in cities with good air service, negative r's (low distance, high growth) indicate fast growth in "air" cities.

The best simple r's are shown. One more reminder: unless the text indicates an exception, all r's are based on the over-10,000 sample, with GRO-2:0 as the dependent variable.

Variable	Southeast	Southwest	South
AIR > 40:30	−.41		
AIR > 40:25		−.17	−.28

Like the chi-square tests, the simple correlation tests show air service to be significant in the Southeast and South—now at better than the 1 percent level. The Southwest's simple r is not significant for the over-10,000 sample, used above. However, the over-5,000 sample does give the Southwest a significant simple r when GRO-% is substituted for GRO-2:0 as the dependent variable. In this case, a dummy air variable has an r of −.19. Based on 120 cases, it is significant at the 1 percent level. (The dummy, AIR-1:0, is valued at one in cities more than 35 Interstate-System miles or 25 regular highway miles from an airport.)

The simple r's for air service are deceptively low. Cities that lack air service tend to be unimportant, nonmanufacturing cities: −.55 intercorrelations between air variables and MFG > 0 arise in both the Southeast and the Southwest. Poor air service is thus offset by the pull of noncompetitive labor markets. Holding constant TRADE in the Southeast or MFG > 0 in the Southwest and South gives these partials for—respectively by region—AIR > 40:30, AIR > 25, and AIR > 40:25:

Variable	Southeast	Southwest	South
AIR dummy	−.47	−.41	−.36

All three partials are well above the 1 percent level. The Southeast partial becomes −.42 if MFG > 0 instead of TRADE is controlled. The Southwest partial remains at −.41 if VA ≥ 5 instead of MFG > 0 is held constant. Using VA ≥ 5 in place of MFG > 0 brings the South's partial to −.40.

The standardized partials for AIR > 30 (Southeast) and AIR > 25 (Southwest and South) are as follows:

Variable	Southeast	Southwest	South
AIR dummy	–.55	–.53	–.44

These r's are even farther above the 1 percent significance level than the preceding one-variable-constant r's; air service very definitely has a significant relationship to growth.

Interpretation. The relationship of air service to growth must be regarded as primarily causal—in the sense of air service causing growth. A continuing trend toward regional decentralization of industry—toward production becoming geographically prorated according to population—has created a need for efficient transportation between branch plants and company headquarters. Where long distances are involved, air travel nowadays is generally the most if not the only satisfactory alternative. A 1965 study found that 82 percent of all business trips over 500 miles and 85 percent of all nonautomobile business trips of any distance were by air.[3] Locations that cannot be reached conveniently by air are clearly at a disadvantage. This knowledge brings out the implications of one finding of an interview study covering new plants in the South: "Several company executives indicated that an important element in selecting a new manufacturing plant location was the ease of access to general headquarters and to other plants of the concern."[4]

Other studies provide direct evidence that air service affects plant location. A Texas plant location consultant reports that it is not uncommon for site selection teams in the Southwest to look for commercial air service.[5] One questionnaire survey, which asked company officials to check factors that would be important in selecting "the specific area or site" for a new plant, had "near airport" checked in 20 percent of the replies.[6] "Near airport," in the context of "site," could be interpreted to mean on the same side of town as the airport in a city that has its own airport; how many other respondents would have checked "within 30 miles of an airport"? Another questionnaire survey that did not include air service in its location factor checklist (such surveys rarely do) nevertheless elicited a number of responses favoring proximity to airports.[7]

The possibility exists, of course, that some of the relationship is due to growth's generating a need for air service. We saw that cities with air service tend to have manufacturing. Did manufacturing lead to air service? Obviously, 1960–70 growth could not cause 1960 air service; that sort of reverse causation can be ruled out. Factors that caused pre-1960 growth could have led to both air service and post-1960 growth in some cases. However, holding G:50–60 (1950–60 growth rate) constant actually increases the r's for AIR, making common causation unlikely. Although there certainly are instances where new manufacturing influenced a Civil Aeronautics Board decision to approve air service for a city, causation seems to run primarily from air service to growth.

Table 6-2
Frequency of Cases by Distance to Interstate System

Distance and Service	Southeast		Southwest		South	
	Fast	Slow	Fast	Slow	Fast	Slow
Distance						
21 miles or more	7	16	16	15	23	31
9 to 20 miles	2	3	4	5	6	8
0 to 6 miles	20	10	9	9	29	19
Total Cities	29	29	29	29	58	58
Type of Service[a]						
No Hwy, No Air	3	15	8	13	11	28
Air, No Hwy	6	4	12	7	18	11
Hwy, No Air	6	5	5	5	11	10
Hwy and Air	14	5	4	4	18	9
Total Cities	29	29	29	29	58	58

[a]Cities within 6 miles of Interstate System interchanges have highway service. Cities within 25 miles (Southwest) or 30 miles (Southeast) of a commercial airport have air service.

Interstate System Highways

Previous research also indicates that cities with superior highway service tend to grow faster, at least east of the Mississippi Valley.[8] Superior highway service refers to the Interstate System of limited-access freeways. The Interstate System provides an objective criterion for identifying cities with advantageous highway facilities. Accordingly, the basic highway variable is HWY, distance in road miles from city center to the nearest Interstate System interchange.

Chi-Square Tests. Table 6-2 compares the fast and slow cities in terms of distance to the nearest Interstate System interchange. The lower part of the table provides a different categorization of transport service, combining highways with air service. This second breakdown controls the interference caused by air service in some nonhighway cities and by highways in some cities without air service.

The table shows that Interstate System cities generally do grow faster, but— this agrees with prior research findings[9] —only in the Southeast. In the Southeast, twice as many fast as slow cities lie within 6 miles of the Interstate System. If all Southeast cities more than 6 miles from an interchange are combined into one interval to provide a two-interval breakdown, χ^2 is 5.60. This is significant at better than the 2 percent level.

The 6-mile cutoff is used because six is a natural breaking point: no sample cities are located 7 or 8 miles from Interstate highways. But if the cutoff is lowered to 5 miles for the Southeast, admittedly a questionable procedure, we get this result:

Distance	Fast	Slow	Total
6 miles and up	9	22	31
0 to 5 miles	20	7	27

Now χ^2 is 9.98, well above the 1 percent level. The new cutoff has no noteworthy effect for the Southwest.

The lower part of the table demonstrates that highways would show a stronger relationship to growth if air service were held constant. Among the 29 Southeast cities without air service ("No Air"), only 3 of 18 that also lack Interstate highways are fast-growing. But 6 of 11 that are on the Interstate System show fast growth. If the two middle categories are combined to provide a three-interval breakdown (neither, one, or both), χ^2 is 12.69 for the Southeast. This is significant at the 1 percent level.

Correlation Tests. The best highway correlations came not from HWY but from variables derived from it. Best in the Southeast was 1/logHWY(0.8). This is the reciprocal of the logarithm of HWY, except that its value is constant at 0.8 (1/log16) for distances of 16 miles or more. The constant describes a growth-distance relationship in which growth ceases to decrease with increasing distance beyond 15 miles. *Positive r's for this and other reciprocals are equivalent to negative r's for HWY.* The best Southwest variable was HWY > 8, a 1–0 dummy. For the overall South, SE × HWY-σ had the best simple r. HWY-σ describes growth as proportional to the height of a normal probability curve (percentage of maximum ordinate) at various distances when the curve's standard deviation (σ) is five miles. HWY-σ is high where HWY is low, so positive r's indicate high growth in highway cities. SE × HWY-σ is HWY-σ multiplied by the 1–0 Southeast-Southwest dummy, which zeroes out the Southwest cities and thereby treats highways as unable to discriminate between fast and slow in the Southwest. SE/HWY, a similar variable, has the best standardized partial for the South. The best simple r's for highways are shown below:

Variable	Southeast	Southwest	South
1/logHWY(0.8)	+.39		
HWY > 8		−.00	
SE × HWY-σ			+.22

These r's are consistent with the chi-square findings. For the Southeast, +.39 is safely above the 1 percent level. The Southwest's −.00 is totally insignificant. The +.22 reading for the South is above the 5 percent level but obviously gets all its strength from the Southeast.

More effective control of geographic unevenness in the highway relationship is achieved by holding SE-SW (Southeast-Southwest dummy) constant. This gives SE/HWY a partial of +.27 for the South. Now r is .03 above the 1 percent level.

The standardized partials are considerably higher. Again, it should be understood that 1/logHWY (0.8) and SE/HWY are high where HWY and HWY > 8 are low: positive r's for the reciprocals are equivalent to negative r's for HWY. The partials:

Variables	Southeast	Southwest	South
1/logHWY(0.8)	+.57		
HWY > 8		−.33	
SE/HWY			+.37

The first and third partials are considerably above the 1 percent level; the Southwest partial exceeds the 5 percent level. What is it in the Southwest's standardized control set that, held constant, lifts highways to significance? More than anything else it is the hidden factors that G:50–60, prior growth, is a proxy for. If G:50–60 alone is held constant, HWY > 8 moves from −.00 to −.13; when G:50–60 is controlled last in stepwise correlations with the standardized control set, HWY > 8 moves from −.21 to −.33.

Interpretation. The link between highways and growth surely involves a causal relationship running from highways to growth. Studies dealing with regional (contrasted with local) factors influencing plant location have repeatedly shown that markets is the leading factor.[10] Industry is moving closer to its markets, primarily by setting up branch plants to serve regional markets. The main force behind this decentralization has been transportation.[11] The growth of trucking since the 1930s has greatly improved the cost advantage of short hauls. When railroads were supreme, high terminal costs and low line-haul costs prevented substantial transport savings from decentralization: the terminal costs could not be avoided, and the line-haul savings were small. But trucks, with their low terminal costs and terminal time savings averaging 48 hours, are ideal for short hauls of a few hundred miles. Regional plants now bring important shipping benefits. These benefits depend on highways.

Against this background, it would be quite surprising if industry did not pay some attention to highways when choosing specific locations (cities) within regions. And in fact, plant location studies always place either markets or transportation—or both— at or near the top when the relative importance of *local* factors influencing plant location is assessed;[12] rarely is another factor in first place. Markets and transportation are almost like two sides of a coin: time and cost savings in shipping finished goods are the main reason for locating close to markets. Questionnaire items are invariably too ambiguous to establish whether words like "proximity to highways" mean a plant site immediately adjacent to the main highway, a modern two-lane highway in good repair serving the city, or a city located on the Interstate System. Likewise, one seldom knows whether "markets" is a reason for locating in the region or for choosing the city. Nevertheless, the dominant role of freight transportation creates a strong impression that many companies value the time and cost savings that Interstate System locations offer.

Reverse causation—growth causing the highways—is not a valid alternative explanation for the findings. It simply is not true that Interstate roads were located so as to serve fast-growing nonmetropolitan cities. Rather, they were designed to provide direct links between important metropolitan areas. Some deviations from reasonably straight intermetropolitan connections exist because of topography, or to serve important—but not necessarily fast-growing—cities along the way, or to incorporate older highways, or (rarely) because of political manipulation. But neither past nor projected future growth rates for intervening cities were considered in laying out the routes. Nonmetropolitan cities on the Interstate System are there because they happened to be in the right place. As a matter of fact, one finds a negligible -.09 intercorrelation between G:50–60 and HWY for the Southeast and a striking "wrong sign" intercorrelation of +.33 for the Southwest: Southwest cities on the Interstate system, which started to become operational in the 1960s, actually tended to have slow growth in the 1950s.

The findings do permit doubt about whether Interstate highways have had much effect in the Southwest. But the marginal significance of the Southwest findings does not undermine, and may even strengthen, the Southeast findings. For the present study's findings are remarkably similar to those of a previously mentioned study.[13] That study used a matched-pairs methodology to compare manufacturing growth rates in Interstate and non-Interstate cities. The Interstate cities grew significantly faster only in the East—corresponding to the Southeast in the present study—and on the West Coast. A plausible explanation is that high population density (heavy traffic) and hilly or mountainous terrain (hills and curves) impede movement on regular highways more in the East and on the West Coast than elsewhere. Southeastern textile mills and apparel sewing operations might also be a factor: the combination of trucking and southeastern locations enables them to keep in closer contact with garment centers in the New York area, with trucking needs probably helping the Interstate cities.[14]

Navigable Waterways

The nation's inland and intracoastal waterways provide barge service for firms that need or can benefit from it. The principal waterways in the South are the Mississippi-Ohio River system, including its Cumberland River and Tennessee

River branches; the Mobile-Tombigbee-Warrior system in Alabama; some relatively short coastal rivers in other states; the Gulf Intracoastal Waterway; and the
Atlantic Intracoastal Waterway. Most navigable waterways are controlled to
depths of 9 feet or more, but some are under 9 feet. The hypothetical attraction
of waterway locations was tested with the variable WATER. It is a three-value
dummy using two to designate depths of 9 feet or more, one to designate shal-
lower but still navigable channels, and zero to designate all other locations.

Chi-Square Tests. Table 6–3 compares the proportions of fast and slow cities
with barge service. Because the over-10,000 sample has so few waterway cities,
the usual over-10,000 comparison is supplemented with one for the over-5,000
sample. Both comparisons deny that waterway cities tend to grow faster. In
fact, one sees a faint tendency in the other direction. The over-5,000 sample even
offers, for the Southeast, a chi-square reading that describes the slower growth
among the deep-channel waterway cities as being significant at the 10 percent
level. This finding apparently reflects the decline of some of the old river cities.
Their economies, based on water traffic, have slumped in parallel with a long-run
decline in the importance of water transportation. Flood hazards along major
rivers could also be a factor.

It is true that the over-5,000 sample also shows six fast compared to three
slow deep-channel cities in the Southwest. But this difference is quite insignificant and is not repeated in the over-10,000 sample. Examination of specific cases
in the over-5,000 sample shows that four of the six fast-growing deep-channel
cities in the Southwest are Gulf Coast cities. Their fast growth could be due to
coastal amenities. In any case, three of five Mississippi River cities in the Southwest are slow.

Table 6–3
Frequency of Cases by Waterway Status

Waterway Status	Southeast		Southwest		South	
	Fast	Slow	Fast	Slow	Fast	Slow
Over-5,000 Sample						
Water: 9 ft. and up	5	13	6	3	11	16
Water: under 9 ft.	2	1	1	1	3	2
Nonwaterway	63	56	53	56	116	112
Total Cities	70	70	60	60	130	130
Over-10,000 Sample						
Water: 9 ft. and up	3	4	3	3	6	7
Water: under 9 ft.	1	1	1	2	2	3
Nonwaterway	25	24	25	24	50	48
Total Cities	29	29	29	29	58	58

Correlation Tests. The simple and standardized partial correlation tests for WATER confirm that barge service is not a significant influence. The simple r's for both samples are:

Sample	Southeast	Southwest	South
Over 10,000	–.03	–.03	–.04
Over 5,000	–.14	+.09	–.04

The negative signs indicate a tendency for slow growth to be associated with waterway status: low growth, high depth. As with chi-square, the Southeast reading for the over-5,000 sample is actually significant at about the 10 percent level. But since the sign is wrong, this is not cause for speculation that waterways influence growth.

Could it be that a latent waterway influence is obscured by overlapping influences that push growth in the opposite direction? The standardized partials give only the faintest support to this idea. The partials for the over-5,000 sample are based on sets of control variables similar but not identical to those described in chapter 2 for the over-10,000 sample. The partials:

Sample	Southeast	Southwest	South
Over 10,000	–.02	+.10	+.04
Over 5,000	–.07	+.15	–.02

Both Southwest r's now have the right sign. However, neither is significant at even the 10 percent level, which is ±.25 for the over-10,000 sample and ±.16 for the over-5,000 sample.

Interpretation. Barge service, although undoubtedly of value to particular industries, has no significant effect on growth rate variations. It is used mostly for a limited group of commodities—chiefly coal, sand and gravel, crushed rock, grain, petroleum and petroleum products, chemicals, fertilizer, iron and steel products, and paper and paper products. Also, most barge shipments involve raw materials; water transportation is too slow for general use with finished goods. Waterway shipments are thus relatively unimportant in the overall transportation picture.

Even if the insignificant but positive partial r's for the Southwest result from a waterway stimulus, that stimulus might not be barge service. Many industries that locate along waterways are attracted by benefits other than navigation. Cheap hydroelectric power has attracted industries to the Tennessee River. Some industries need water for cooling and other industrial purposes. And, alas, our rivers are often used to dispose of industrial waste.

An unpublished Department of Commerce study, conducted in 1964, suggests that nontransportation considerations generally outweigh barge service in inducing plants to locate on rivers. The study looked at ten large plants in ten industries along the Ohio River. Only two made heavy use of barge transportation: a thermal electric plant got most of its coal by water, and a petroleum refinery received most of its crude oil and shipped out substantial quantities of refined products by water. But nine of the ten plants used the river for industrial water.

Notes

1. Leonard F. Wheat, "The Effect of Airline Service on Manufacturing Growth in Cities Below 40,000 Population" (Washington, D.C.: Economic Development Administration, 1970), pp. 1-37.

2. Ibid, pp. 24-29.

3. John B. Lansing, *The Travel Market: 1964-65* (Ann Arbor: University of Michigan, Survey Research Center, 1965), p. 40.

4. Glenn E. McLaughlin and Stefan Robock, *Why Industry Moves South* (Washington, D.C.: National Planning Association, 1949), p. 93.

5. T.E. McMillan, Jr., "Why Manufacturers Choose Plant Locations vs. Determinants of Plant Locations," *Land Economics* 41 (August 1965): 243.

6. Ibid., p. 242.

7. James F. McCarthy, *Highways, Trucks, and New Industry* (Washington, D.C.: American Trucking Associations, 1963), pp. 29, 93-96, 100-107.

8. Leonard F. Wheat, "The Effect of Modern Highways on Urban Manufacturing Growth" (Washington, D.C.: Economic Development Administration, 1969), pp. 1-37.

9. Ibid.

10. Leonard F. Wheat, *Regional Growth and Industrial Location: An Empirical Viewpoint* (Lexington, Mass.: D.C. Heath, 1973), pp. 6-20, 21, 183-89, 208-9.

11. Benjamin Chinitz and Raymond Vernon, "Changing Forces in Industrial Location," *Harvard Business Review* 38, no. 1 (January-February 1960): 126-36.

12. See, for example, McMillan, "Locations," p. 242; McCarthy, *Highways,* p. 30; and Eva Mueller and James N. Morgan, "Location Decisions of Manufacturers," and Melvin L. Greenhut and Marshall R. Colberg, "Factors in the Location of Florida Industry," in Gerald J. Karaska and David F. Bramhall, eds., *Locational Analysis for Manufacturing* (Cambridge, Mass.: MIT Press, 1969), pp. 64, 66, 208, 212.

13. Wheat, "Highways."

14. See Robert M. Lichtenberg, *One-Tenth of a Nation* (Cambridge, Mass.: Harvard University Press, 1960), pp. 115, 148; Victor R. Fuchs, *Changes in the Location of Manufacturing in the United States Since 1929* (New Haven: Yale University Press, 1962), p. 25; Harvey S. Perloff, Edgar S. Dunn, Jr., Eric E. Lampard, and Richard F. Muth, *Regions, Resources, and Economic Growth* (Washington, D.C.: Resources for the Future, 1960), p. 420 ("there is some advantage in being close to the New York market to provide quick delivery on special orders"); and McLaughlin and Robock, *South,* p. 34 (citing a textile company's desire to be within twenty-four-hour shipping time of New York, its principal market).

7

Education

Education levels might cause, represent other factors that cause, or be caused by growth. Climbing enrollments in colleges and universities—plus concomitant increases in college, retail, and service employment—contribute to population growth. Colleges might also attract industry, but any such effect is likely to be minor. Lower education (elementary and secondary) is more apt to influence plant location: better educated workers, particularly skilled workers, might be sought by industry. Education could also be a proxy for rural-urban characteristics that attract or repel industry. Or, a positive relationship between growth and education could express causation running from growth to education: in-migration by better educated workers, who are more mobile, could raise educational levels in fast-growing cities—at least in the Southwest, where there is less demand for unskilled rural workers.

Higher Education

The basic college variable is COL-5. It is valued at 5 for cities with state universities, 4 for other Ph.D. schools, 3 for master's degree schools with at least 2,000 students, 2 for other master's degree schools and bachelor's degree schools of at least 1,000, 1 for smaller bachelor's degree schools and those junior colleges with at least 500 students, and 0 for anything else (including all seminaries). Each city is rated according to its highest-level college or university.

Chi-Square Tests. Table 7-1 distributes the fast and slow cities among three higher education categories. An initial distribution using all six of COL-5's categories showed only one slow city among the three highest categories, so these three categories were combined. (The exception was a nonmajor Ph.D. school.) The initial distribution also showed no appreciable fast-slow differences between the junior college and no-college categories, so they were also combined. Because there are very few college towns in the over-10,000 sample—too few for chi-square testing in the Southeast—the over-5,000 sample is included in the table.

Even before the tables were prepared, it was obvious that colleges would be significant. The over-5,000 sample has five cities in category 5 (state university). The schools are the University of Virginia, the University of Georgia, the University of Mississippi, the University of Arkansas, and the Oklahoma State University of Agriculture and Applied Science. Four of the five cities where they are located

Table 7–1
Frequency of Cases by Higher Education Status

Status	Southeast		Southwest		South	
	Fast	Slow	Fast	Slow	Fast	Slow
Over-5,000 Sample						
Advanced Degree	11	0	12	1	23	1
Four-year	2	1	5	1	7	2
J.C. or none	57	69	43	58	100	127
Total Cities	70	70	60	60	130	130
Over-10,000 Sample						
Advanced degree	6	0	8	1	14	1
Four-year	2	1	3	1	5	2
J.C. or none	21	28	18	27	39	55
Total Cities	29	29	29	29	58	58

have the highest growth rates in the sample for their respective states; the fifth ranks second. All of four category-5 schools in the over-10,000 sample rank first among the sample cities from their states.

When we get to the table, the findings are wholly convincing. In the over-5,000 sample, 23 of 24 advanced-degree cities and 7 of 9 four-year cities are fast-growing. Chi-square was computed by combining these two categories to provide a two-interval breakdown. The result is χ^2 values significant at the 1 percent level for all three regions: 9.60 for the Southeast, 12.26 for the Southwest, and 22.78 for the South.

In the over-10,000 sample, 14 of 15 advanced-degree cities and 5 of 7 four-year cities are in the fast column. This time χ^2 is 6.34 for the Southwest and 12.62 for the South, based on the same two-interval breakdown. The first figure is significant at about the 1.5 percent level, the second at well above the 1 percent level. A Southeast χ^2 of 4.74 is technically invalid because there are less than ten cases (nine) in the top interval.

Correlation Tests. Several college variables, including a 1–0 (college-noncollege) dummy, were tested. The highest r's came from COL-4, COL-3, and their square roots. COL-4 combines COL-5's two lowest categories, giving no credit to junior colleges and going to a 4–3–2–1–0 scale. COL-3 further combines the two highest categories, valuing both at 3. For simplicity, the exhibits mention only COL-3— most often the best. The simple r's for both dependent variables are:

Variable	Southeast	Southwest	South
COL-3 (with GRO-2:0)	+.35	+.37	+.36
COL-3 (with GRO-%)	+.40	+.43	+.42

Even when GRO-2:0 is the dependent variable, COL-3 is significant at the 1 percent level in all three regions. With GRO-% as the dependent variable, the r's are far above the 1 percent level. Incidentally, because GRO-% uses the augmented (fast-moderate-slow) sample with half again as many cities, the 1 percent level is lower than with GRO-2:0. The Southeast's +.40 and the Southwest's +.43 compare with a 1 percent level of ±.28; the South's +.42 compares with a 1 percent level of ±.20.

College towns tend to differ from other cities in their characteristics. As a result, the college factor is duplicated when other factors are held constant. In particular, holding air service constant lowers the significance of colleges: college towns tend to have air service. The duplication is greater in the Southwest if air service and manufacturing are jointly held constant, since air service is not itself significant enough to have much effect until manufacturing is controlled. The following partials hold constant AIR $>$ 30 in the Southeast, AIR $>$ 25 and MFG $>$ 0 in the Southwest, and AIR $>$ 25 in the South.

Variable	Southeast	Southwest	South
COL-3 or $\sqrt{\text{COL-3}}$	+.22	+.27	+.29

The Southwest and South partials are still significant—at the 1 percent level for the South—but the Southeast's +.22 is insignificant.

Still lower partials for the Southwest and South result with the standardized control sets. The standardized partials:

Variable	Southeast	Southwest	South
COL-3 or $\sqrt{\text{COL-3}}$	+.35	+.14	+.27

Now the Southeast's +.35 and the South's +.27 reach the 2 percent and 1 percent levels, respectively, although the Southwest's +.14 is insignificant. The Southwest partial becomes significant at +.29 if AIR $>$ 25 and MFG $>$ 0 are left out of the standardized control set.

Interpretation. The college findings are easy to interpret. Rising college enrollments contribute directly and indirectly to population growth—directly because college students are counted as residents of their college communities for census purposes and indirectly because college faculty and administrative employment and community retail and service employment go up when enrollments go up. The obvious conclusion is that growth results from colleges.

Theoretically, of course, COL-3 could be a proxy for air service and other factors. But cities with air service are not almost invariably fast-growing, whereas college cities are. Proxy characteristics could make a small contribution to COL-3's excellent performance but cannot be the principal explanation. Moreover, since the standardized partials for the Southeast and South are significant even with air service and numerous other important factors held contsant, proxies are out of the question.

On the other hand, it is unlikely that colleges will affect growth as much in the 1970s as they did in the 1960s. College enrollment increases were abnormally high in the 1960s. Degree-credit student enrollment rose 57 percent between 1950 and 1960 but 121 percent between 1960 and 1970; the ten-year percentage increase more than doubled in the 1960s. This phenomenal increase was partly due to the wartime and early postwar baby boom of the 1940s: these babies reached college age in the 1960s. Another factor was the Vietnam war, which led many students to enroll—or continue on into graduate school—in order to avoid military service. As the draft tapered off and then ceased, enrollments began to level off. The period 1970–73 witnessed a 6 percent increase in enrollments, compared to a 25 percent increase for the 1960–63 period. A 1970–80 increase of only 15 percent is projected by the U.S. Office of Education—a far cry from the 121 percent increase of the 1960s.[1]

Lower Education

Elementary and secondary school education is described by two variables: HI-SCH (percentage of high school graduates among persons over twenty-five) and SCHOOL (percentage of children in school, ages fourteen to seventeen). Intended to describe more or less the same thing, these variables actually differ widely in their chi-square and correlation behavior. Some of the difference results because HI-SCH, but not SCHOOL, tends to act as a proxy for colleges—at least when colleges is not held constant. For the South, COL-5 has an intercorrelation of +.45 with HI-SCH but of only +.07 with SCHOOL. In fact, COL-5 and SCHOOL have a negative intercorrelation of −.10 for the Southeast; their Southwest intercorrelation is +.13. This preliminary evidence suggests that HI-SCH but not SCHOOL may be a proxy for colleges.

Chi-Square Tests. Table 7–2 compares the fast and slow cities in terms of their distributions over several lower education categories. Under the SCHOOL breakdown (lower half of the table), one of the otherwise equally wide intervals is subdivided to show a significant cutoff point for differentiating between fast and slow cities.

HI-SCH shows strength in both subregions but especially in the Southeast. There χ^2 is 4.44, significant at the 5 percent level, when based on two intervals: above and below 38 percent. For the Southwest, a three-interval breakdown with 38–42 percent as the middle interval gives a χ^2 of 5.40. This is a little short of the 5 percent level. When the same three-way breakdown is used for the over-

Table 7-2
Frequency of Cases by Lower Education Status

Status	Southeast		Southwest		South	
	Fast	Slow	Fast	Slow	Fast	Slow
HI-SCH						
53% or more	1	0	4	0	5	0
43% to 52%	6	1	7	4	13	5
38% to 42%	11	8	10	10	21	18
33% to 37%	5	15	3	6	8	21
32% or less	6	5	5	9	11	14
Total Cities	29	29	29	29	58	58
SCHOOL						
90% or more	0	1	10	8	10	9
86% to 89%	8	13	10	14	18	27
84% to 85%	3 } 12	8 } 11	1 } 3	0 } 0	4 } 15	8 } 11
82% to 83%	9	3	2	0	11	3
78% to 81%	7	3	3	4	10	7
77% or less	2	1	3	3	5	4
Total Cities	29	29	29	29	58	58

all South, χ^2 is 12.32; under a two-way breakdown, χ^2 is 7.78. Both readings exceed the 1 percent level.

These findings, however, are heavily influenced by colleges. Whereas the Southeast has only nine college towns, five of them are among the eight cities where the high school percentage is 43 percent or more. Seven of thirteen college towns in the Southwest are among the fifteen cities with high school percentages of 43 percent or more. For both subregions combined, three of the five cities in the highest interval have colleges.

SCHOOL, which does not overlap the college factor, shows radically different behavior. In the Southeast, high educational levels go with *slow* growth. This relationship is significant at the 1 percent level: χ^2 is 7.04, based on a comparison of cities at or above 84 percent in school with those below 84 percent. In the Southwest, this negative relationship does not prevail, but neither does the positive relationship found with HI-SCH: the Southwest shows no discernible relationship between growth and schooling.

Correlation Tests. The correlation tests add a dummy, SCHOOL $\geqslant$ 84, to the basic variables. It is valued at one where the percentage of children in school equals or exceeds 84 percent and at zero elsewhere. So that the link between colleges and the high school percentage can be seen more clearly, the findings shown repeat the r's given earlier for COL-3. The simple r's, with GRO-2:0 as the dependent variable, are as follows:

Variable	Southeast	Southwest	South
COL-3	+.35	+.37	+.36
HI-SCH	+.30	+.31	+.30
SCHOOL	−.27	+.01	−.10
SCHOOL ≥ 84	−.38	−.04	−.22

Note that HI-SCH is again significant but that it is slightly lower than COL-3 in its r's. COL-3's higher r's, together with its very clear causal relationship to growth, indicates that any proxy relationship has COL-3 providing the substance. Meanwhile, SCHOOL continues to be independent of the others. The dummy's −.38 reading for the Southeast reaches the 1 percent level; the South's −.22 stands at about the 2 percent level. Thus SCHOOL is significantly negative despite COL-3's being significantly positive.

Before looking at the standardized partials, we need to view some non-standardized ones that drop the college variables from the standardized control sets. These allow one more comparison of COL-3 and HI-SCH. For COL-3 in the Southeast and South, the partials are actually the standardized ones; but for the Southwest, where SCHOOL must be dropped from the control set, COL-3's partial is not the standardized one. The Southeast partial for SCHOOL uses the dummy. The partials:

Variable	Southeast	Southwest	South
COL-3	+.35	+.24	+.27
HI-SCH	+.25	+.25	+.16
SCHOOL	−.25	+.39	+.10

Once more, HI-SCH is generally close to, but lower than, COL-3. HI-SCH is behaving like a college proxy. Though HI-SCH's partial is higher than COL-3's in the Southwest, this is explained by HI-SCH's further intercorrelation with SCHOOL. SCHOOL, in turn, looks like anything but a proxy. In the Southeast, it is still negative. In the Southwest, it is significantly positive, and at the 1 percent level. SCHOOL's Southwest r, unlike HI-SCH's, does not depend on COL-3's, for COL-3 is not only considerably lower but insignificant. SCHOOL, it seems, has latent significance in the Southwest.

The standardized partials, which simply add the college variables to the control sets used above, complete the picture. As before, the Southeast r opposite SCHOOL actually comes from SCHOOL ≥ 84. The Southwest r's, including the one for HI-SCH, naturally drop SCHOOL from the control set. The standardized partials:

Variable	Southeast	Southwest	South
HI-SCH	+.16	+.08	+.08
SCHOOL	−.19	+.36	+.10

For HI-SCH, the result is expected: holding colleges constant drives HI-SCH back toward zero. In other partial correlation experiments, HI-SCH occasionally became significant in the Southwest despite control of colleges. But in these instances, HI-SCH was following SCHOOL, which always had a higher positive r—just as it has in the preceding partial correlations. This proxy relationship results from a +.47 Southwest intercorrelation between HI-SCH and SCHOOL, compared to one of only +.18 in the Southeast.

For SCHOOL, the partials involve what looks like a contradiction. SCHOOL is negative in the Southeast yet positive and significant—at the 2 percent level— in the Southwest. Does this point to spurious correlation? Or is there a logical explanation?

Interpretation. SCHOOL could conceivably speak for what it superficially describes: eduation. But this is unlikely. Although plant location surveys reveal occasional interest on the part of manufacturers in "good schools," this desire is in the context of amenities. Industry is thinking of its employee's children, not of a well-educated work force. Furthermore, if education per se were what SCHOOL represents, SCHOOL's correlations with growth would probably be positive in the Southeast as well as the Southwest.

A more promising explanation flows from the Southeast-Southwest contrast shown by SCHOOL. This contrast brings to mind an earlier one found with manufacturing. That contrast saw E_m/E, which apparently represents labor-intensive manufacturing, becoming significantly negative in the Southeast but not in the Southwest. Southeastern cities with high levels of labor-intensive industry have low growth rates because, it was deduced, this industry is generally slow-growing and also has adverse effects on local labor markets. Labor-intensive industry is a significant factor only in the Southeast because that is where most of it goes. It goes there because wages are generally lowest there and because high rural population density in the Southeast provides adequate labor supplies in small cities and rural areas, where the very lowest wages are found. Southwestern industry is more capital-intensive; E_m/E is correspondingly insignificant in the Southwest.

The key point here is that many, if not most, new plants in the Southeast seek comparatively rural locations. The object is cheap labor. But cheap labor goes hand in hand with other rural characteristics, among them low taxes and low educational achievement. The connection between cheap labor and poor education is of primary concern. Very likely, SCHOOL is a proxy for wages in the Southeast: low schooling signifies low wages, which in turn bring high growth rates by attracting labor-intensive industry. Secondarily, SCHOOL could also be a proxy for taxes. As will be explained later, however, the tax influence is not too strong in the Southeast.

SCHOOL's significantly positive partial r's for the Southwest indicate high growth in cities with high percentages of children in school. High levels of schooling go with relatively urban locations. The explanation, then, could be that new plants are favoring the more urbanized places. Rural locations are less popular in the Southwest not only because low wages are less important to its type of industry (capital-intensive) but because southwestern rural areas are often too thinly populated to provide adequate labor supplies. (The Southeast-Southwest contrasts in growth rates for cities of 5,000 to 10,000, as shown in tables 4-1 and 4-2, are suggestive in this respect.) A related consideration is that capital-intensive industry has more demand for skilled labor. Skilled labor is easier to find in relatively urban cities—and sometimes is a product of schooling.

Two other possible interpretations, which tend to contradict each other, involve reverse causation. In the Southeast, where low education goes with high growth, it could be that abundant jobs in fast-growing cities lure the young out of school and into the work force. Though plausible, this hypothesis is weak. To begin with, it is not at all clear that fast growth means abundant jobs for four-teen- and fifteen-year olds or even sixteen- and seventeen-year olds, whereas SCHOOL looks at children in the fourteen-to-seventeen age bracket. Also, if this explanation is correct, why does it not apply in the Southwest too?

The other possibility is that, through a migration mechanism, growth raises the level of schooling. Mobility rates are higher for the better educated workers.[2] In-migration resulting from job opportunities in fast-growing cities should therefore tend to raise the percentages of children in school—assuming that better educated parents generally keep their children in school longer. If fast growth in one decade continues in the next, high in-school percentages resulting from growth in one period will be linked to fast growth in the next. Though contradicted by the Southeast findings, this explanation probably has some validity for the Southwest. The Southwest states have lower rural population percentages, and the region's relatively capital-intensive industry generates less demand for unskilled rural workers. Therefore, in-migration in the Southwest should draw less on unskilled and poorly educated rural workers.

Most likely, causation runs both ways in the Southwest: education (or at least the urbanization for which it stands) attracts industry, and new industry attracts better educated families.

Notes

1. Percentage increases computed from U.S. Office of Education, *Digest of Educational Statistics, 1973* (Washington, D.C.: Department of Health, Education, and Welfare, 1974), table 8, p. 74, and from a revised 1980 projection of 9,907,000 provided by W. Vance Grant of the Office of Education's National Center for Educational Statistics; the revised projection supersedes one of

10,905,000 published in U.S. Office of Education, *Projections of Educational Statistics to 1981-82* (Washington, D.C.: Department of Health, Education, and Welfare, 1973), table 5 (column 3), p. 23.

2. John B. Lansing and Eva Mueller, *The Geographic Mobility of Labor* (Ann Arbor: Survey Research Center, University of Michigan, 1967), p. 43.

8 Labor: Wages and Skill

Any of several labor factors might promote growth by attracting industry. These factors include low wages, the availability of skilled labor, an abundant general labor supply, and weak unions. The importance of wages has already been mentioned in connection with manufacturing and education; this chapter provides a more direct and detailed analysis of the hypothetical wage influence. Skilled labor, not yet discussed, merits consideration because some industries require skills that are not widely available in nonmetropolitan cities. The general labor supply and unions, factors often mentioned in plant location surveys, must be passed over, however: no suitable variables for testing their significance are available. (Population, examined earlier, is theoretically useful as a labor supply variable; but the negative partial r's generated by POP are not consistent with the idea that it makes a good proxy for labor supply.)

Wage Levels

A good wage variable is hard to find. Average hourly and weekly wages are published for states but not for cities. The best city data are 1960 median annual earnings for four occupational groups. One group, "operatives and kindred workers," seems more representative of factory workers than the others. Also, the median earnings of operatives are less apt to reflect unemployment, as opposed to hourly wages, than are the earnings of laborers, the next best group. The basic wage variable is therefore the median annual earnings of operatives and kindred workers, abbreviated EARN.

Chi-Square Tests. Table 8-1 compares the wage level distributions for the fast and slow cities, using the EARN concept of wages. The "absolute scale" in the top half of the table uses actual median earnings. The "relative scale" in the lower half relates median earnings for each city to the median for all cities in the state, as computed from the augmented over-10,000 sample. This latter comparison classifies earnings as being either more than $200 above the median (rounded to the nearest $100), within $200, or more than $200 below. The relative scale recognizes that wage levels differ from state to state and also between Southeast and Southwest: a wage that is absolutely high (or low) by subregional or regional norms might be relatively low (or high) in the state context.

The absolute scale shows that, in both subregions, cities with median earn-

71

Table 8-1
Frequency of Cases by Wage Level

Median Earnings	Southeast		Southwest		South	
	Fast	Slow	Fast	Slow	Fast	Slow
Absolute Scale						
$3,250 or more	3	6	8	16	11	22
$3,000 to $3,249	4	2	3	3	7	5
$2,500 to $2,999	13	11	9	6	22	17
Under $2,500	9	10	9	4	18	14
Total Cities	29	29	29	29	58	58
Relative Scale						
$201 above median	7	14	9	16	16	30
Within $200 of median	15	7	6	8	21	15
$201 below median	7	8	14	5	21	13
Total Cities	29	29	29	29	58	58

ings for "operatives and kindred workers" of $3,250 or more are generally slow-growing: both subregions show exactly twice as many slow as fast cities at $3,250 and up. These differences are not significant in either subregion, because the highest interval has too few cases. But for the overall South, if the three lowest intervals are treated as one—this gives a two-way breakdown—χ^2 is 4.24, significant at the 5 percent level.

The relative scale offers even greater fast-slow contrasts. For the Southeast, if the two lowest intervals are combined to provide a two-interval breakdown, χ^2 is 2.70. This is marginally significant, reaching the 10 percent level. For the Southwest, if the two highest intervals are treated as one, χ^2 is 5.01, significant at about the 3 percent level. For the South, merging the two lowest categories sends χ^2 to 6.01, significant at the 1.5 percent level. The finding of higher significance in the Southwest is unexpected, but wages are beginning to look important.

Before leaving table 8-1, we should observe that the general wage level is substantially higher in the Southwest: it has twenty-four cities above $3,250, compared to nine in the Southeast. This confirms what has been said in earlier analyses about wages being especially low in the Southeast—the explanation given for labor-intensive industry's preference for that subregion. Of course, the finding that wages are lower in the Southeast might seem inconsistent with the chi-square finding that wages are slightly more significant in the Southwest. But, to anticipate, a relatively strong tax influence in the Southwest reinforces wages enough to explain this discrepancy.

Correlation Tests. The correlation tests employ EARN, three dummies based on EARN, and a secondary wage variable, SKIL/P. The dummies are EARN ⩾

3,000, EARN $\geqslant$ 3,250, and EARN $\geqslant$ 3¼:3; the last is a 2-1-0 dummy valued
at two where EARN reaches $3,250, one where EARN reaches $3,000 but not
$3,250, and zero elsewhere. SKIL/P is skilled workers per capita, where "skilled"
means craftsmen, foremen, and kindred workers (a census category). Intended
for measuring skilled labor supplies, SKIL/P seems to serve better as a proxy for
wages. Its consistently and often significantly negative r's refute the idea that it
describes a skilled labor attraction. Wages should be low where SKIL/P is low
because (1) skilled labor gets higher wages and (2) low SKIL/P probably reflects
low manufacturing employment and correspondingly low labor market competition. Though it generally moves up and down with EARN in partial correlation
tests, SKIL/P sometimes shows evidence of duplicating VA $\geqslant$ 5 and $\sqrt{\text{COL-3}}$ as
well; so it must be interpreted with extreme caution.

The simple r's for EARN (used generically hereafter to represent any variant
that yields the highest r in a given context) and SKIL/P follow:

Variable	Southeast	Southwest	South
EARN	−.14	−.29	−.21
SKIL/P	−.17*	−.21	−.19*

The r's marked with asterisks (*) use GRO-%, which provides a better fit, in
place of GRO-2:0 as the dependent variable. The Southeast r's are not significant.
But EARN's −.29 in the Southwest and −.21 for the South are both three points
above the 5 percent level. SKIL/P's −.19 for the South also exceeds the 5 percent
level. The negative signs mean, of course, that growth is high where wages are
low.

The surprisingly low simple r's, most notably the −.14 for EARN in the
Southeast, are due to interference by other factors. Racial mix interferes the
most. RACE $\geqslant$ 33:20, a 2-1-0 racial mix dummy, and EARN have intercorrelations of −.47 for the Southeast, −.28 for the Southwest, and −.34 for the South:
the nonwhite percentage runs high where wages are low. High nonwhite percentages apparently contribute to slow growth (more will be said about this in
chapter 11) and thereby offset the industrial pull of low wages. If RACE $\geqslant$
33:20 is therefore held constant, these partials result:

Variable	Southeast	Southwest	South
EARN	−.28	−.35	−.28
SKIL/P	−.28	−.29	−.26

For EARN, these r's reach the 5 percent level for the Southeast and the 1
percent level for the Southwest and South. In the Southeast, other interference
comes from air service, which tends to be lacking where wages are low. If AIR $>$
30, in addition to RACE $\geqslant$ 33:20, is held constant, EARN's Southeast partial
climbs to −.34, significant at the 1 percent level. Air service is not a factor in the

Southwest: holding both RACE $\geq$ 33:20 and AIR $>$ 25 constant gives EARN a partial of −.34.

The standardized partials provide more complete control covering not only racial mix but other factors that might interfere. The result:

Variable	Southeast	Southwest	South
EARN	−.35	−.25	−.25
SKIL/P	−.16	−.34	−.21

Here EARN is significant at the 2 percent level for the Southeast and at the 1 percent level for the South. EARN is not significant in the middle column, but SKIL/P is. SKIL/P's −.34 for the Southwest stands at about the 2 percent significance level.

The standardized partials actually overcontrol by holding constant property taxes per capita, which partly duplicates wages. Because wages and taxes both tend to be low in comparatively rural cities, EARN and TAX/P have intercorrelations of +.33 for the Southeast, +.46 for the Southwest, and +.49 for the South. If the tax variables are therefore removed from the standardized control sets, these semistandardized partials result:

Variable	Southeast	Southwest	South
EARN	−.43	−.36	−.31
SKIL/P	−.29	−.39	−.26

Now EARN is significant at the 1 percent level for the Southeast and South and at the 2 percent level for the Southwest, where SKIL/P gets to the 1 percent level. These r's admittedly undercontrol, allowing wages to function partly as a proxy for taxes. But they do suggest that the wage factor is quite significant.

Interpretation. Contradictions and ambiguities in the findings require further consideration, however, The principal contradiction is that theory says that the wage influence should be strongest in the Southeast, where manufacturing is relatively labor-intensive, whereas the chi-square and simple correlation findings are more significant in the Southwest. This contradiction begins to dissolve, however, when we observe that EARN—the truest measure of wages—has partials of −.34 in both subregions when race and air service are controlled. And the contradiction vanishes when the standardized partials are viewed: EARN becomes more significant in the Southeast. One other consideration is that EARN has a higher intercorrelation with TAX/P in the Southwest. EARN therefore gains more in the Southwest from its secondary role as proxy for TAX/P—which is why EARN goes up only .08 in the Southeast but .11 in the Southwest when TAX/P is removed from the standardized control sets.

The ambiguities arise mostly from duplication between wages and taxes. EARN's simple r's and preliminary partials—those which hold just RACE $\geq$

33:20 constant—clearly get a lot of support from the tax sector. For example, when just TAX/P is held constant, EARN goes from -.14 (simple r) to -.08 in the Southeast and from -.29 to -.09 in the Southwest. But the standardized partials, which also have taxes held constant, show wages to be significant in its own right. Again, the Southeast's best multiple correlation combination (chapter 14, table 14-2), which uses eleven variables to reach the highest R obtainable with significant variables, includes both a tax and a wage variable; both are significant at the 1 percent level.

In the Southwest, it must be admitted, the standardized partial for EARN is not significant; only the semistandardized one that drops TAX/P from the standardized control set is. But other control combinations can be found under which both TAX/P and EARN are significant. An example is the Southwest's best six-variable multiple correlation combination (table 14-3). It includes both TAX/P and EARN $\geq 3,000$, with both reaching the 1 percent significance level. TAX/P is the more significant variable in this combination, and just about all partial correlation tests agree. This is what one would expect: the Southwest's relatively capital-intensive industry should be more concerned about taxes than wages. But the wage factor does seem to have a degree of independent significance in the Southwest.

Another ambiguity stems from duplication between wages and manufacturing. This is a problem mainly in the Southwest. There the strongest wage variable, SKIL/P, represents not only wages but a residual manufacturing influence that registers in VA ≥ 5 even when MFG > 0 is controlled. SKIL/P and VA ≥ 5 generally move up and down together in stepwise partial correlation tests. The control set that gives SKIL/P its standardized partial of -.34 gives VA ≥ 5 a partial of -.39. If SKIL/P is added to the control set, VA ≥ 5 drops to -.28; if VA ≥ 5 is added instead, SKIL/P drops to -.21.

SKIL/P, then, is partly a proxy for manufacturing; it identifies nonmanufacturing cities. But if nonmanufacturing cities are attractive because of low wages and noncompetitive labor markets, as seems to be the case, the wage element in SKIL/P is not seriously alloyed. Moreover, in the above mentioned situation where VA ≥ 5 is added to the standardized control set, EARN actually creeps up from -.25 (standardized partial) to -.27. This is still .03 below the 5 percent significance level; but duplication of EARN by TAX/P, held constant, explains this deficiency.

On balance, and with theoretical expectations considered along with the evidence, it appears that the wage factor *is* an influence in the Southwest but not as much as in the Southeast.

Skilled Labor Supplies

SKIL/P was originally intended for testing the hypothesis that skilled labor contributes to growth by attracting industry. Unfortunately, this variable behaved as a proxy for wages and other factors, showing a negative instead of a positive relationship to growth. A related variable, SKILL, is still available, though. SKILL is the total number of skilled workers—craftsmen, foremen, and kindred workers— in a city. Because it was regarded as too much of a proxy for population, SKILL was not used for correlation tests. But chi-square results are available.

Chi-Square Tests. Table 8–2 categorizes the fast and slow cities according to how many skilled workers they have. We are looking for a predominance of fast cities in the highest categories. Any strong tendency for cities with abundant skilled labor to grow fast could not be due to size, for high population involves no such strong tendency.

The cities with many skilled workers do not show faster growth. On the contrary, one finds a very mild tendency in the other direction. It is strongest in the Southwest. There all five cities with under four hundred skilled workers are fast-growing. The five-zero split involves too few cases for statistical significance. But if the tendency is genuine, it probably represents the attraction of nonmanufacturing cities: all five cities have MFG ratings of zero.

Interpretation. The skilled labor hypothesis must be tentatively rejected— tentatively because of the dubious quality of the skill variable and in view of the limited amount of testing. This is not to deny that skilled labor is probably an attraction for metropolitan areas. Cohn's study of industry in the Pacific Northwest emphasizes skilled labor's role in attracting industry to a metropolis: "Outside of Seattle, Portland, Spokane, and Tacoma the labor supply is inadequate both qualitatively and quantitatively. Most of the secondary centers have populations between 10,000 and 40,000. A manufacturer cannot expect to find many skilled workers in so small a labor pool. He must lure them from Seattle and Portland."[1]

Lichtenberg draws similar findings from a study of the interaction between national forces and economic growth in the New York region. He notes that among labor-oriented industries, "industries relying heavily on unskilled labor

Table 8–2
Frequency of Cases by Number of Skilled Workers

Number	Southeast		Southwest		South	
	Fast	Slow	Fast	Slow	Fast	Slow
1,000 or more	8	7	8	10	16	17
600 to 999	8	12	8	11	16	23
400 to 599	10	8	8	8	18	16
Under 400	3	2	5	0	8	2
Total Cities	29	29	29	29	58	58

have a markedly different locational pattern from those whose location is governed by skilled labor." Plants requiring unskilled labor at rock-bottom wages have gone to the South—especially southern rural areas—and to rural areas elsewhere. Industries oriented toward skilled labor, however, are concentrated in metropolitan areas. There they benefit "from being near other plants that make extensive use of skilled labor, for they thus have flexibility to hire people when they need them and lay them off when they do not."[2]

But the present study is not concerned with factors that might cause metropolitan cities to grow faster or slower than nonmetropolitan ones; it deals with growth rate variations within the nonmetropolitan sector. Skilled labor could well be unimportant to those firms that choose to locate outside of metropolitan areas. And it might be less important in the South than in other regions: southern industry is more labor-intensive and relies more on unskilled labor. McLaughlin and Robock found in their interview survey of eighty-eight new plants in the South that, "although some of the new plants wanted semiskilled or highly skilled workers, the emphasis on securing trained workers has not been great."[3] One reason for this was that improved training techniques developed during World War II have "made it possible to train green workers quickly."[4] Another interview study, this time covering only twenty-eight plants in four southern cities and towns, found that "when firms came in search of labor, they looked for labor available at low wage rates, rather than for specified skills."[5]

It is certainly plausible, then, that skilled labor is undermined as a locational influence in the nonmetropolitan South by two factors: (1) a preference for metropolitan areas by those firms that do have important skilled labor requirements and (2) a relative lack of demand for skilled labor on the part of southern industry.

Notes

1. Edwin J. Cohn, Jr., *Industry in the Pacific Northwest and the Location Theory* (New York: Kings Crown Press, Columbia University, 1954), p. 46.

2. Robert M. Lichtenberg, *One-Tenth of a Nation* (Cambridge, Mass.: Harvard University Press, 1960), pp. 48–56, esp. pp. 48, 53, 54.

3. Glenn E. McLaughlin and Stefan Robock, *Why Industry Moves South* (Washington, D.C.: National Planning Association, 1949), p. 69. Cf. Victor R. Fuchs, *Changes in the Location of Manufacturing in the United States Since 1929* (New Haven: Yale University Press, 1962), pp. 124–25.

4. McLaughlin and Robock, *South,* p. 69.

5. Abt Associates, Inc., *The Industrialization of Southern Rural Areas* (Washington, D.C.: Economic Development Administration, Contract No. 7-35482, 1968), p. 17.

9

Property Taxes

Survey research on plant location often points to local taxes as a factor influencing plant location. This makes sense: taxes, like wages, are part of the cost of doing business, and cost minimization is a basic locational consideration. Yet one can easily be skeptical, for local taxes—and particularly tax *differences* between cities—are a relatively minor element in total costs. Survey responses affirming a tax influence can be motivated by self-interest. An intermediate possibility is that capital-intensive firms but not labor-intensive ones are concerned about taxes: property taxes bear more heavily on plants that rely more on equipment in place of labor. Whatever the truth, the widespread interest in taxes as a factor affecting growth makes the hypothetical tax influence worth investigating.

Property Tax Significance Tests

A good tax variable is as hard to find as a good wage variable. Tax statistics are not available for cities below 25,000. County taxes must therefore be used. But county taxes are infuenced not only by the sample cities but by occasional other cities and by varying proportions of rural population and area, which have lower tax rates. Another problem is that published county tax figures cover property taxes only, although the heavy reliance of local governments on property taxation lessens this problem. For better or for worse, then, county property taxes were used to compare tax burdens. The variable is TAX/P, or county property taxes per capita.

Chi-Square Tests. Table 9–1 compares the TAX/P distributions for the fast and slow cities. The absolute scale in the upper half of the table has distortion resulting from tax level variations between states and regions: cities that are high or low by subregional or regional standards may actually be different relative to other cities in their own states. The relative scale, constituting the lower part of the table, attacks this problem. It classifies cities according to whether their per-capita property taxes are $3 or more above their state median, within $2, or $3 or more below. The state median is based on the augmented (fast-moderate-slow) sample.

The absolute scale shows almost no sign of a tax influence in the Southeast. True, there is a 4:1 fast-slow ratio for five cities with taxes of less than $20 per

79

Table 9-1
Frequency of Cases by County Property Taxes per Capita

Per-Capita Taxes	Southeast		Southwest		South	
	Fast	Slow	Fast	Slow	Fast	Slow
Absolute Scale						
$50 or more	4	5	7	14	11	19
$45 to $49	5	2	1	4	6	6
$40 to $44	1	5	7	7	8	12
$30 to $39	9	7	10	2	19	9
$20 to $29	6	9	4	2	10	11
Under $20	4	1	0	0	4	1
Total Cities	29	29	29	29	58	58
Relative Scale						
$3 above median	9	15	5	15	14	30
Within $2 of median	7	6	10	8	17	14
$3 below median	13	8	14	6	27	14
Total Cities	29	29	29	29	58	58

capita; but when the next highest interval is also considered, one finds equal numbers of fast and slow cities—10 fast and 10 slow—for all cities below $30.

The Southwest, however, has a strong tendency for low-tax cities to grow fast: there are 14 fast but only 4 slow cities with per-capita taxes below $40, compared to 8 fast but 18 slow cities with taxes above $45. If a three-interval breakdown is used, with $40 to $44 as the middle interval, the Southwest's fast-slow differences exceed the 1 percent level: χ^2 is 9.40

For the South, χ^2 is 4.19, significant at better than the 5 percent level, when based on a two-interval breakdown dividing at $40.

The relative scale uncovers hidden differences in the Southeast and sharpens the fast-slow contrast for the overall South. The Southeast differences still lack significance, but a 9:15 fast-slow ratio in the highest interval points to latent significance. The Southwest differences are still significant, this time at the 2 percent level: χ^2 is 6.18, based on a two-interval breakdown. And for the South, when the two lowest intervals are merged, the resulting two-way breakdown sends χ^2 to 8.24. This is considerably better than the 1 percent level.

The chi-square findings show, then, that low-tax locations have significantly faster growth in the Southwest but only slightly faster growth in the Southeast. At the same time, the Southeast has most of the low-tax locations: the Southeast has twice as many cities—36 compared to the Southwest's 18—below $40. Taxes are less related to growth where taxes are lowest. Is this because industry has less incentive to avoid taxes where taxes are generally low to begin with?

Correlaton Tests. Simple correlations reiterate the chi-square findings: TAX/P is

significant in the Southwest but not in the Southeast. The new findings use
TAX/P and a dummy, TAX/P $\geq$ 40, which is valued at one where TAX/P equals
or exceeds $40 per capita. The simple r's:

Variable	Southeast	Southwest	South
TAX/P	-.06	31*	-.17
TAX/P $\geq$ 40	-.07	-.37	-.21

The r of -.31 for the Southwest, marked with an asterisk, substitutes GRO-%
for GRO-2:0 as the dependent variable. Based on eighty-seven cases (instead of
fifty-eight), this r is significant at better than the 1 percent level. When GRO-2:0
is the dependent variable, TAX/P gets only to -.27 in the Southwest; but
TAX/P $\geq$ 40, as shown above, reaches -.37, again above the 1 percent level.

One might suspect that, as was the case with wages, racial mix is causing
interference. Are taxes, like wages, low where the nonwhite percentage is high?
Such a tendency is present, but it is weaker than the comparable tendency found
with wages. Holding racial mix constant has almost no effect in the Southeast.
In the Southwest, when GRO-2:0 is the dependent variable, controlling RACE
$\geq$ 20 has a slight effect: TAX/P goes from -.27 to -.34, but TAX/P $\geq$ 40 climbs
just one point to -.38.

Something else is interfering, though, and that something is air service:
cities with low taxes tend to lack air service. If AIR > 30 (Southeast) or AIR >
25 (Southwest and South) is controlled, these r's result:

Variable	Southeast	Southwest	South
TAX/P	-.14	-.31	-.22
TAX/P $\geq$ 40	-.24	-.42	-.28

The South as well as the Southwest now has TAX/P $\geq$ 40 reaching the 1
percent significance level. The Southeast partial has climbed by .17 but is still a
little short of significance.

The standardized partials take care of the Southeast and provide more significant readings for the other two regions as well. The r's:

Variable	Southeast	Southwest	South
TAX/P	-.39	-.45	-.34
TAX/P $\geq$ 40	-.44	-.37	-.39

This time the highest partials in all three columns exceed the 1 percent significance level. Even so, the significance of taxes may be slightly understated; for
the standardized control sets include wage variables. Just as taxes duplicates
wages, so does wages duplicate taxes. If the wage controls are dropped, these
partials result:

Variable	Southeast	Southwest	South
TAX/P	-.46	-.49	-.39
TAX/P $\geqslant$ 40	-.49	-.38	-.42

Whereas the standardized partials overcontrol, these undercontrol; the tax variables are getting some proxy support from wages. Somewhere between these semistandardized r's and the standardized r's is where the tax variables probably belong.

Problems of Interpretation

Given the a priori expectation of slow growth in high-tax cities, one is tempted to infer that high taxes inhibit growth. But with taxes, extraordinary caution in interpreting is needed: taxes are linked with a number of other factors that are, in turn, related to growth. Outstanding among these other factors are (1) wages, (2) other factors with rural-urban variations, (3) singular local conditions, and (4) fast growth in the recent past.

Taxes and Wages. As already observed, TAX/P and EARN have intercorrelations of +.33 for the Southeast, +.46 for the Southwest, and +.49 for the overall South. Taxes are higher in urban and other high-income areas, and particularly in or near metropolitan areas. Urbanization means higher public facility and service requirements; facilities and services require taxes. Taxes are also influenced by the tax base, which varies with wealth and income—major determinants of property values. Wages, meanwhile, also run higher in urban areas and, of course, are closely related to wealth and income. The upshot is that property taxes and wages are generally high or low in the same places. This makes it hard to tell a tax effect from a wage effect.

Nevertheless, it seems probable that TAX/P is mostly a proxy for wages in the Southeast. It is well known that low wages have attracted labor-intensive industries, most notably the textile industry, to the Southeast. Fuchs, in his analysis of 1929–54 manufacturing shifts, finds that the comparative gains of the South Atlantic states rested heavily on textiles, the nation's most labor-intensive industry; comparative gains in the East South Central states were predominantly in textiles and in apparel, the fourth most labor-intensive industry.[1] This knowledge justifies a presumption that wages have influenced locational decisions at the local, as well as the regional, level. Correspondingly, plant location surveys have generally ranked wages ahead of taxes in locational importance—despite the temptation for businessmen to give self-serving answers when asked how taxes affected their decisions. Another point: property taxes are less of a burden in the Southeast, less apt to be of concern. One reason for this is that labor-intensive industry is relatively important in the Southeast, which means there is less machinery and equipment to tax. Another is that property tax levels are generally lower in the Southeast. And for the many Southeast plants going to rural areas, outside city limits, taxes should generally be too low for significant advantages to be realized near alternative cities.

The Southwest probably has TAX/P speaking more for itself—that is, for taxes instead of wages. Labor has not been so important in the comparative gains of the Southwest, where the biggest gains have been in such capital-intensive industries as chemicals, aircraft, machinery, and petroleum.[2] These industries should be more concerned about taxes: they have more taxable property. Regarding chemicals, McLaughlin and Robock observe: "Chemical plants require large capital investments. Consequently, property taxes are a relatively important cost of operation."[3] Also, to repeat an earlier point, low rural population densities in the Southwest push industry toward relatively urbanized areas. Such places have generally higher tax rates, which should cause more concern.

Other Rural-Urban Factors. Other factors besides wages and taxes have rural-urban variations. TAX/P could be a proxy for one of these. Is it? TAX/P's intercorrelations with POP are remarkably close to zero: +.06 in the Southeast and −.002 in the Southwest. Population, therefore, could not form a bond between TAX/P and something else. But another facet of urbanization—namely, metropolitan area proximity—might. A striking finding is that taxes tend to be higher in places close to large or fast-growing metropolitan areas. This phenomenon applies mainly in the Southeast, where the intercorrelations shown arise. (The four metropolitan area variables are defined in chapter 2.)

Variable	D_m	P_m	G_m	$P_m G_m / D_m$
TAX/P	−.16	+.33	+.54	+.60

The last partial, +.60, expresses a gravity relationship wherein taxes are directly proportional to the population and growth rate of the nearest major metropolitan area and inversely proportional to its distance away. Comparably high r's are not found in the Southwest, except that there is one of +.34 relating TAX/P to G_m. (TAX/P's weaker relationship to metropolitan area proximity in the Southwest may result from high property tax levels in oil-producing cities in West Texas—a subject coming up shortly. These high-tax cities are remote from any major metropolitan area, and this brings the D_m intercorrelation around to positive: +.37.)

So, taxes are related to metropolitan area proximity. And other factors that are characteristically high (or low) in metropolitan areas are likely to have similar relationships to metropolitan area variables. Some of these factors, such as business services, probably attract industry and thereby promote growth. But let us focus on three that hurt metropolitan area growth: land costs, construction costs, and unionization. All three are high in metropolitan areas and low in rural areas. And all three could be functions of the size, growth rate, and distance of the nearest major metropolitan area. For example, Berry has shown that the average value of farm land and buildings generally declines as one proceeds along gradients running from Detroit, Chicago, Minneapolis, and Duluth, with lesser peaks occurring in the vicinity of smaller metropolitan areas along the way.[4]

Is it possible that TAX/P is behaving as a proxy for land costs, construction costs, and unionization? It certainly is possible. But it seems unlikely as far as any important effects are concerned. For one thing, plant location surveys have not revealed much concern about land and construction costs, although these factors are sometimes considered. Unionization is more frequently mentioned, sometimes under such euphemisms as "worker attitudes." However, if unionization were related to TAX/P through metropolitan area proximity, and if unionization were at the same time significantly related to growth, then the "metro" variables should themselves be significantly related to growth—as proxies for unionization. But, as we shall see in the next chapter, the "metro" variables do not reach significance in the Southeast, the region where TAX/P has a strong "metro" relationship. And in the Southwest, the standardized partials for TAX/P hold the two strongest "metro" variables constant.

Singular Local Conditions. Another possibility is that TAX/P reflects industrial situations that underlie fast or slow growth. Only 5 of the 116 cities in the over-10,000 sample were above $100 for TAX/P; only 6 of the 116 were even above $66. All of these high-tax cities were in Texas. And, in each case, taxes were high because of oil and natural gas production. Petroleum resources gave the cities strong tax bases, high total revenue, and correspondingly high per-capita tax revenue. Yet tax *rates* were low. It is most improbable that taxes frightened away any industrial prospects.

These circumstances suggest that TAX/P is partly a proxy for petroleum resources and comparable singularities. Extreme values for a variable can have a disproportionate influence on a correlation—if they happen to match up with the maximum or minimum values for the other variable. When all extreme values relate to a hidden cause, it is possible that that cause is influencing the correlation. In the Texas situation, four of the six high-tax cities are slow-growing. Resource depletion or even stable production levels might explain the slow growth, but negative r's for TAX/P try to put the blame on taxes.

The likelihood that petroleum was the primary factor behind the negative r's for TAX/P is slight, because (1) TAX/P was given a maximum value of $99 when the data was key-punched to reduce the possibility of distortion caused by the extreme cases, (2) the sample had only five of these $99 cases, and (3) two of the six cases above $66 had fast growth. However, if many of the other above-average TAX/P values were influenced by petroleum or similar industrial factors, and if slow growth in the affected cities were the rule, it would be wrong to infer that high taxes caused the slow growth.

On balance, the links between petroleum and TAX/P look strong enough to support an inference that TAX/P is secondarily a proxy for petroleum and possible similar industrial factors in the Southwest. In this respect, petroleum acts like wages, which evidently provides even stronger proxy support in the Southwest and is of primary importance in the Southeast. But, as suggested in the analysis of taxes and wages, TAX/P probaly speaks primarily for taxes in the Southwest.

Recent Growth: A final possibility is that low taxes, rather than being a cause of growth, are caused by it. One cannot doubt that, in the long run, continued growth results in new facilities, new and expanded services, and higher wages and salaries (including those paid to governmental employees). Essentially, this is why taxes are higher in large metropolitan areas than in small cities.[5] It is entirely possible, though, that growth will increase a city's property tax base more than it raises costs in the short run. If so, and particularly where growth results from new industry that can assume part of the tax load, per-capita taxes might fall.

The trouble with this reverse causation hypothesis is that it could not very well apply to cities in general. In individual cases, per-capita taxes might indeed decline following growth. This would mainly be in cases where existing facilities—schools, public works, and so on—had enough excess capacity to absorb the additional demands imposed by growth. Relatively fixed costs could then be spread over a larger taxpaying population. Other growing cities, however, would need to expand their facilities and services; bond levies and generally higher governmental overhead would bring higher per-capita taxes. At the same time, the occasional practice of granting temporary tax exemptions or other tax concessions militates against any short-run drop in taxes when new plants arrive. All things considered, *higher* per-capita taxes as a result of growth must be the dominant tendency. If it were not, metamorphosis from small city to metropolitan area would not lead to the observed outcome: higher property tax levels.

Comparative intercorrelations between TAX/P and two growth variables support the idea that growth raises rather than lowers taxes. The growth variables are G:50-60 (1950-60 percentage growth) and GRO-% (1960-70 percentage growth); the augmented sample is used. For the Southeast, where taxes appear to be a relatively weak influence, both intercorrelations are close to zero. But the Southwest findings are enlightening:

Variable	G:50-60	GRO-%
TAX/P (1960)	+.05	−.31

Going by the −.31 *r* between 1960 TAX/P and 1960-70 growth, we can assume that a comparable *r* would be found between 1950 TAX/P (not actually tested) and 1950-60 growth. That would mean that places with high 1950-60 growth had generally low 1950 taxes. But these places no longer had generally low taxes in 1960: the +.05 r between 1960 TAX/P and G:50–60 reveals a neutral relationship, even a faint tendency for places with high 1950–60 growth to have high 1960 taxes. The implication is that taxes went up—not down—in many of the places that had fast growth in the 1950s.

It should be added that the standardized partial of -.45 for TAX/P in the Southwest has G:50–60 held constant. If G:50–60 is removed from the standardized control set, r falls from -.45 to -.39. This further refutes the idea that TAX/P is a proxy for prior growth or whatever caused it.

Notes

1. Victor R. Fuchs, *Changes in the Location of Manufacturing in the United States Since 1929* (New Haven: Yale University Press, 1962), pp. 23–25, 202–18, 235.

2. Ibid., pp. 25, 218–22, 235–36.

3. Glenn E. McLaughlin and Stefan Robock, *Why Industry Moves South* (Washington, D.C.: National Planning Association, 1949), pp. 101–2. Cf. The Fantus Company, Inc., *The Appalachian Location Research Studies Program: Summary Report and Recommendations* (prepared for the Appalachian Regional Commission, Contract No. C-273-66) (New York: December 1966), p. 20: "For the capital intensive industry, taxes on machinery and equipment obviously are a great deal more important than real estate taxes."

4. Brian J.L. Berry, *Growth Centers in the American Urban System,* vol. 1 (Cambridge, Mass.: Ballinger, 1973), pp. 82–89.

5. See Advisory Commission on Intergovernmental Relations, *State-Local Taxation and Industrial Location* (Report A-30) (Washington, D.C.: 1967), p. 68. Cf. McLaughlin and Robock, *South,* p. 100.

10 Metropolitan Area Proximity

There is a suspicion among economists—almost a conviction with some—that cities located relatively close to major metropolitan areas tend to grow faster, particularly where the metropolitan area is itself fast-growing. The terms "filter-down," "hierarchical diffusion," and "spillover growth" are used. These depict growth as concentrating in metropolitan areas and spreading to nearby cities. Hoover and Thompson believe that new industries locate in metropolitan areas to obtain needed skills but, as processes become routinized and skill needs decline, the now-mature industries disperse to places with lower wages or closer markets.[1] Berry, the chief exponent of filter-down, adapts this idea. He argues that innovations, such as television, are diffused on a larger-to-smaller basis.[2] "Growth occurs as a consequence of the filtering of innovations downward through the urban hierarchy and the spread of use of the innovations among consumers residing within the urban fields of the adopting centers."[3] The process might be aided by rising wages in large cities and the "imitation" of large-city entrepreneurs by small-city ones.[4] Another possibility is that metropolitan factories attract suppliers to nearby cities or else farm out certain labor-intensive operations to branch plants in rural areas. Or, rather than actual diffusion, there might be common causation: metropolitan and hinterland cities might both react to the same regional markets, resources, climate, and topography. But whatever the mechanism, if any, growth in hinterland cities should be inversely proportional to distance from the metropolis and directly proportional to its size and growth rate.

Distance to Metropolitan Area

This study defines major metropolitan areas as those with 1960 SMSA (Standard Metropolitan Statistical Area) populations of 250,000 or more according to 1970 area delineations. If a proximity influence exists, a hinterland city probably responds more to a large SMSA than to a smaller one located just a little closer. Proceeding from a theoretical gravity relationship, the study uses the simplified formula P_m/D_m^2 to select the SMSA with the highest potential for influencing a sample city. P_m is the SMSA's 1960 population, and D_m is its central city's distance from the sample city (the subscript m stands for metropolitan). Only in a few instances was the farthest of the two SMSAs chosen. D_m, measured in road miles, is the basic distance variable.

87

Chi-Square Tests. Table 10–1 shows the metropolitan distance distributions for the fast and slow groups. Both the over-5,000 and the over-10,000 sample are covered—for two reasons: first, the over-5,000 sample suggests a critical distance (80 miles) not corroborated by the over-10,000 sample and, second, there is unusually high interest in the spillover hypothesis.

The over-5,000 sample suggests a spillover-type relationship for the Southwest but not for the Southeast. Actually, both subregions show higher proportions of slow than fast cities at distances over 200 miles. But this difference, involving ten fast compared to seventeen slow cities for the overall South, is not even close to significance. What *is* significant is the Southwest's pattern of thirty-two fast but only fourteen slow cities within 80 miles of a central city. (Eighty miles is the optimal cutoff, providing maximum differentiation.) Note that both intervals within 80 miles follow this pattern and that all four intervals above 80 miles are the opposite—more slow cities than fast. With the Southwest's cities thus assigned to two broad intervals—above and below 80 miles—χ^2 is 10.18. This is well above the 1 percent significance level.

The over-10,000 sample exhibits similar growth patterns, except for the 80-mile cutoff. One finds the same tendency for the over-200-mile cities in both subregions to grow slowly and for relatively close-in cities to grow faster in the Southwest but not the Southeast. The over-200-mile findings, though involving too few cases for significance, now present very sharp contrasts: one fast and six slow cities beyond 200 miles for the South. Although the 80-mile cutoff no longer applies, significant differences do arise when a 160-mile cutoff is used. We

Table 10–1

Frequency of Cases by Distance to Nearest Major SMSA

Distance	Southeast		Southwest		South	
	Fast	*Slow*	*Fast*	*Slow*	*Fast*	*Slow*
Over-5,000 Sample						
201 miles or more	2	5	8	12	10	17
161 to 200 miles	7	3	3	5	10	8
121 to 160 miles	7	9	10	11	17	20
81 to 120 miles	21	14	7	18	28	32
41 to 80 miles	23	32	26	12	49	44
40 miles or less	10	7	6	2	16	9
Total Cities	70	70	60	60	130	130
Over-10,000 Sample						
201 miles or more	0	2	1	4	1	6
161 to 200 miles	5	4	1	5	6	9
121 to 160 miles	4	2	8	3	12	5
81 to 120 miles	8	2	9	6	17	8
41 to 80 miles	7	14	9	7	16	21
40 miles or less	5	5	1	4	6	9
Total Cities	29	29	29	29	58	58

find two fast but nine slow cities more than 160 miles from an SMSA. For a two-interval (above and below 160) test, χ^2 is 4.04, significant at the 5 percent level.

The Southwest findings nevertheless give less support to the proximity hypothesis than first appearances suggest. Looking at just the four intervals within 160 miles in the over-10,000 sample, we see that the proportion of fast cities increases with each increment of distance. In the closest interval—40 miles or less—there are actually four slow cities compared to one fast city. Fast cities strongly preponderate only in the 121-to-160-mile interval. In other words, it might hurt to be more than 160 miles from an SMSA, but inside the 160-mile range it does not seem to help to be extra close to the metropolis. Since the benefits of nearness do not attenuate gradually with increasing distance, the evidence is more indicative of a handicap attached to faraway cities than of growth spilling over from the metropolis.

Because the 80-mile cutoff works only with the over-5,000 sample, it seems possible that just the smallest cities—those of 5,000 to 10,000—benefit from close proximity. This possibility was tested by subdividing the over-5,000 sample's Southwest cities into those above and those below 10,000. (Geographic comparability between the fast and slow cities suffers when this is done.) For the below-10,000 cities, 56 percent of thirty-four fast cases but only 26 percent of thirty-one slow cases were within 80 miles. But the larger cities had about the same fast-slow ratio for cases within 80 miles: 50 percent fast and 21 percent slow. Cities of 5,000 to 10,000 do not seem to have any special relationship with SMSAs.

Correlation Tests. The correlation tests for distance use the basic distance variable, D_m, and several derived variables, such as $1/D_m$. The highest r's for the Southwest and South come from two dummies, $D_m > 160$ and $SW \times D_m > 160$. $D_m > 160$ is valued at one for cities more than 160 miles from a metropolis and at zero elsewhere; $SW \times D_m > 160$ uses a Southwest-Southeast dummy (1–0) multiplier to zero out the Southeast cities, where D_m's negative relationship to growth does not hold. The simple r's (asterisks mark those based on GRO-%) are as follows:

Variable	Southeast	Southwest	South
D_m	+.08	−.27*	−.14*
$D_m > 160$	−.04	−.37	−.20
$SW \times D_m > 160$	.00	−.37	−.25

As with chi-square, the Southeast shows no clear relationship. But the other tests reveal significant relationships of the expected type. D_m's −.27 for the Southwest, based on the augmented sample, almost reaches that sample's 1 percent level (±.28); $D_m > 160$'s r of −.37, though based on the regular fast-slow sample, is above the 1 percent level. So is the −.25 value reached by $SW \times D_m$

> 160 for the South. This last r, of course, rests wholly on the Southwest cities; $SW \times D_m > 160$ cannot discriminate among the Southeast cities, which are all valued at zero.

The standardized partials confirm the significance of metropolitan area proximity in the Southwest and raise interesting questions about a possible reverse relationship in the Southeast. The partials are:

Variable	Southeast	Southwest	South
D_m	+.27	−.22	−.06
$D_m > 160$	+.08	−.47	−.21
$SW \times D_m > 160$	.00	−.47	−.31

Although D_m's +.27 partial for the Southeast is not significant, it certainly demands attention: it is within .02 of significance yet is opposite in sign from the −.47 partial in the Southwest column. This strongly refutes the hypothesized proximity relationship where the Southeast is concerned. And it seems to affirm that this region's manufacturing is rural-oriented: the fast-growing cities tend to be remote (D_m is high) from major metropolitan areas.

The Southwest and South again tell a different story—the story of low growth where distance is high. All r's in the last two columns are negative: low growth, high distance. And the highest in each column are significant at the 1 percent level. The findings, then, support the proximity hypothesis as applied to the Southwest.

It should be added that the Southwest partials are not weakened by the use of another "metro" variable, $P_m G_m$ (population-weighted growth rate), in the Southwest control set. On the contrary, $D_m > 160$'s Southwest partial is only −.42 if $P_m G_m$ is removed from the control set.

Interpretation. There is a definite and significant tendency for cities located relatively close to major SMSAs to grow faster, but only in the Southwest. The Southwest-only aspect is consistent with earlier findings. We have seen that the Southeast's industry is relatively labor-intensive. Labor-intensive industries are attracted to the abundant cheap labor found in rural areas. Industry's rural orientation in the Southeast seems to be reflected in that region's negative r's for TRADE, E_m/E, SCHOOL, EARN, and TAX/P; it may also stand behind the relatively (if insignificantly) high growth rates found in tables 4-1 and 4-2 for southeastern cities of 5,000 to 10,000 population. Rural areas—partly as a matter of concept—are farther from major SMSAs. This condition not only neutralizes but overshadows any metropolitan area attraction in the Southeast. But in the Southwest, industry is more capital-intensive, more urban-oriented. A metropolitan-area-distance relationship can overcome neutralizing forces.

This distance relationship might well represent spillover growth—in the general sense of hinterland growth induced by SMSA growth, past and present.

Concerning particulars, Berry's filtering-down-of-innovations theory lacks credibility, as will be explained later. But the metropolitan area could well be a magnet attracting new plants to its general vicinity. The attractions are things known to persuade many firms to locate *within* the metropolis: markets (consumer and industrial), satellite industries (die shops, machine shops, supply houses), equipment maintenance and repair services, financial and other business services, trunkline airports, cultural and recreational amenities, and—for the businessman's wife—shopping facilities. For some firms, high wages and other metropolitan-area liabilities may offset these advantages and lead to compromise locations; places within, say, 100 miles of the metropolis may be selected. Many such places, because they can reach out to metropolitan areas in several directions, can exploit regional markets better than SMSA locations can for particular plants and products.

The over-10,000 findings in table 10-1 indicate the possibility of an inverted U-shaped growth curve: growth rates at first increasing as distance increases and then decreasing at greater distances. Slow growth close to SMSAs could be explained by higher wages, taxes, site costs, and construction costs. At some equilibrium distance (varying with the firm), these disadvantages would become weak enough, and the offsetting disadvantages of remoteness strong enough, for the curve to turn back down.

It is also possible that the proximity relationship is not due to spillover. There might even be a "spillinto" phenomenon: hinterland growth—or decline—affecting the metropolis. To use an example outside the South, the rise and decline of iron mining in northern Minnesota was chiefly responsible for the growth, and more recently the decline, of the Duluth-Superior metropolitan area, located about 80 miles from the center of the Mesabi iron range. Elsewhere, adverse hinterland conditions probably explain not the growth of but the *lack* of a major SMSA close to slow-growing hinterland cities. Both of two slow-growing West Texas cities in the sample are about 350 miles from the nearest major SMSA (Dallas–Ft. Worth). They are located in an arid, somewhat desolate region where a general lack of amenities, together with other adverse conditions, might be the cause of both their stagnation and the failure of a major SMSA to develop. Remote cities in Appalachia are also stagnating, but topography and topographically related cultural factors—not distance to SMSAs—may be their main problems.

From a positive viewpoint, subregional stimuli such as oil and natural gas resources might be causing growth in both the metropolis and the nonmetropolitan cities nearest to it. Imagine a circular resource region with a metropolis located part way between center and edge. Nearby cities in all directions from the metropolis lie within the resource circle of influence. But many of the more remote cities, particularly those in the same direction from center as the metropolis, are outside the circle. And their slow growth is due to being outside the resource circle.

Metropolitan Area Size and Growth Rate

To repeat, any spillover-type benefits to surrounding cities should be directly proportional to the size and growth rate of the metropolitan area. Size, measurable by population, is what gives the metropolis its hypothetical ability to in-influence its hinterland; growth is what spills over, so the amount spilled should increase with the amount available for spilling. Some interaction between the size and growth rate influences is likely: the absolute growth of an SMSA is probably more important than its relative growth when it comes to spillage. These considerations underlie the next three variables tested: P_m (SMSA population, 1960), G_m (SMSA population growth rate, 1960–70), and $P_m G_m$ (population weighted by growth rate). For any sample city, these variables relate to the same SMSA that was used in measuring D_m—the one for which P_m/D_m^2 is highest.

Chi-Square Tests. Table 10–2 compares the numbers of fast and slow cities in different P_m intervals. Both samples are again used. We are looking for a preponderance of fast cities in the highest intervals, particularly in the Southwest. However, neither sample has anything resembling a significant distributional difference between the fast and slow groups. We do see consistently more slow than fast cities in the lowest interval (250,000 to 400,000), but such small differences could easily arise by chance.

Table 10–3 distributes the fast and slow groups according to G_m. Although no sharp contrasts between the fast and slow groups are evident, tendencies are. Both subregions in both samples show more slow than fast cities in the lowest G_m interval and more fast than slow cities in the highest. Though very insignificant, the differences might be larger if P_m were constant.

Table 10–2
Frequency of Cases by Population of Nearest Major SMSA

	Southeast		Southwest		South	
SMSA Population	Fast	Slow	Fast	Slow	Fast	Slow
Over-5,000 Sample						
1,000,000 or more	17	19	22	20	39	39
700,000 to 999,999	14	8	16	18	30	26
400,000 to 699,999	24	23	13	12	37	35
250,000 to 399,999	15	20	9	10	24	30
Total Cities	70	70	60	60	130	130
Over-10,000 Sample						
1,000,000 or more	10	7	7	6	17	13
700,000 to 999,999	5	5	9	11	14	16
400,000 to 699,999	9	9	10	6	19	15
250,000 to 399,999	5	8	3	6	8	14
Total Cities	29	29	29	29	58	58

Table 10–3
Frequency of Cases by Growth Rate of Nearest Major SMSA

SMSA Growth Rate	Southeast		Southwest		South	
	Fast	Slow	Fast	Slow	Fast	Slow
Over-5,000 Sample						
30% or more	17	15	21	20	38	35
20% to 29%	7	5	9	11	16	16
10% to 19%	32	31	26	22	58	53
Under 10%	14	19	4	7	18	26
Total Cities	70	70	60	60	130	130
Over-10,000 Sample						
30% or more	9	5	7	6	16	11
20% to 29%	3	3	7	5	10	8
10% to 19%	10	13	13	13	23	26
Under 10%	7	8	2	5	9	13
Total Cities	29	29	29	29	58	58

No chi-square tests were performed with $P_m G_m$, since it was generated by computer and was available for correlation tests only.

Correlation Tests. The simple correlation findings for metropolitan area size and growth rate give just a little encouragement to the proximity hypothesis. With the over-5,000 sample, all r's for P_m, G_m, and $P_m G_m$ are in the +.05 to –.05 range. But with the over-10,000 sample, a few r's begin to approach significance. Most of the simple r's shown—those marked with asterisks—use GRO-%; it gives slightly better results.

Variable	Southeast	Southwest	South
P_m	+.06*	+.14*	+.09*
G_m	+.15	+.08*	+.08*
$P_m G_m$	+.11	+.18*	+.12*

Though none of these r's is significant, even at the 10 percent level, each bears the expected positive sign.

The standardized partials are another matter: they provide strong support for the proximity hypothesis where the Southwest is concerned. These r's restore GRO-2:0 to its usual position as the dependent variable and, of course, remove $P_m G_m$ from the Southwest control set. The r's:

Variable	Southeast	Southwest	South
P_m	+.16	+.39	+.08
G_m	+.07	+.22	+.02
$P_m G_m$	+.17	+.40	+.06

Again, every r has the right sign—plus. The Southeast r's are still well short of significance. But the +.39 partial for P_m and the +.40 for $P_m G_m$ both reach the 1 percent level. Incidentally, if $D_m > 160$ is removed from the Southwest control set, P_m and $P_m G_m$ decline to respective partials of +.26 and +.34. This means that the relationship between metropolitan and nonmetropolitan growth is partly obscured by distance variations until distance is held constant.

Interpretation. $P_m G_m$'s relationship to growth is probably genuine. This variable has significant partials vis-à-vis both GRO-2:0 and GRO-% in the Southwest. P_m, G_m, and $P_m G_m$ all have the expected sign—plus—in every region. And the findings agree with the D_m findings insofar as the Southwest is the only region where proximity is significantly related to growth.

As with D_m, however, it is uncertain that P_m or $P_m G_m$ describes a spillover phenomenon, hierarchical diffusion, or something of that nature. Quite possibly, hinterland city growth rates relate to metropolitan area population and growth through common causation: subregional assets (or lack of same) affecting both the metropolis and many nearby cities.

The asset most likely to be shared by fast-growing SMSAs and their respective hinterlands in the Southwest is markets. Markets is the leading cause of growth differentials among regions.[5] Strong markets exist where the supply of regionally produced goods (manufacturing) is low relative to demand (population). A supply-demand gap means that goods must be shipped from afar, often from Manufacturing Belt locations in the Northeast. The transportation "tariff" induces outside firms to establish branch plants in the region and protects home industry from outside competition.

Markets are especially strong in the Southwest. The Southwest has comparatively little manufacturing (see table 5-1); it has had considerable in-migration, particularly in Texas, where climate amenities are an attraction; out-migration by blacks is less than in the Southeast; and wage levels (purchasing power) are higher. The resulting supply-demand gap, enhanced by the Southwest's greater distance from Manufacturing Belt factories, has encouraged Manufacturing Belt firms to establish branch plants. Transport savings are the object.[6] Transport savings can generally be maximized by locating at or near the market region's population center of gravity. (This region varies from plant to plant.) The center of gravity tends to be in the vicinity of a large metropolis. The biggest and fastest growing SMSAs in the Southwest are Houston and Dallas–Ft. Worth. They have undoubtedly attracted many market-oriented plants. But some of these plants have gone to smaller cities capable of serving the same markets. Metropolis and hinterland have grown for the same reason.

Natural resources—petroleum and natural gas in particular—could also be shared by both a metropolis and its hinterland cities—and this is certainly true in Texas. It is even possible that resources operate indirectly, via hinterland growth, on the metropolis and thereby entail the "spillinto" growth mentioned earlier.

If common causation is the correct explanation for $P_m G_m$'s significance in the Southwest, it also explains $P_m G_m$'s lack of significance in the Southeast. The Southeast has lots of labor-oriented industry and, therefore, proportionately less market-oriented industry; in fact, the low wages that attract the former undercut consumer demand and thereby deter the latter. Labor-oriented industry does not lend itself to common causation. Low wages may be a region-wide asset in one sense, but they do not benefit metropolitan and nonmetropolitan cities alike: the labor-oriented firms generally prefer nonmetropolitan cities.

Gravity Relationships

If SMSA proximity has several causal facets—distance, population, and growth rate of the SMSA—a gravity formula might best describe the growth relationship between sample city and SMSA. The basic gravity formula, based on the physical analogue of the gravitational attraction between two masses, would in this instance be $(P_m \times POP)/D_m^2$. Or, if we regard the "mass" of the SMSA as its population weighted by its growth, the formula is $(P_m G_m \times POP)/D_m^2$. These formulas assume that a sample city's population (POP) influences the amount of interaction between the cities—as it certainly would if we were dealing with trips between two urban areas. But maybe POP does not affect spillover in the growth situation; maybe P_m/D_m^2, G_m/D_m^2, or $P_m G_m/D_m^2$ is the proper formula. All five formulas plus variations using D_m and D_m^3 in place of D_m^2 were tested.

Correlation Tests. Like $P_m G_m$, the gravity variables were generated by computer and thus were not available for chi-square testing. We therefore begin with simple correlations. The following r's are for the two gravity variables that did best and for a third whose partial r will later be viewed. The gravity hypothesis calls for a plus sign before the r's.

Variable	Southeast	Southwest	South
P_m/D_m	–.02	+.02	–.00
$P_m G_m/D_m$	+.07	–.02	+.02
$(P_m G_m \times POP)/D_m$	+.17	–.00	+.09

None of these r's is significant; the Southwest r's are particularly insignificant; and many of the signs (on these and other gravity variables) are wrong. So far, the gravity hypothesis is not supported.

Do the standardized partials agree that there is no gravity relationship? Yes and no. They agree for the over-10,000 sample. The best-performing gravity variables and their partials follow. The Southwest's partials exclude $D_m > 160$ and $P_m G_m$ from the control set, and the South's partials exclude SW $\times D_m > 160$.

Variable	Southeast	Southwest	South
P_mG_m/D_m	–.08	+.14	+.01
$(P_mG_m \times POP)/D_m$	–.10	+.16	+.03
$(P_mG_m \times POP)/D_m^3$	+.02	–.16	–.02

The best of these r's, the +.16 partial for $(P_mG_m \times POP)/D_m$ in the Southwest, is far short of the 5 percent level ($\pm.29$). And it is even farther below the +.40 reached by P_mG_m alone: introducing interaction between "mass" and distance causes r to fall. (P_mG_m's +.40 standardized partial for the Southwest, unlike $(P_mG_m \times POP)/D_m$'s, holds $D_m > 160$ constant. But if $D_m > 160$ is added to the control set used above, the gravity variable performs even worse, reaching only +.10 instead of +.16.) These findings reject the gravity hypothesis.

Nevertheless, the over-5,000 sample does provide a very significant gravity partial for the Southwest. It comes from $(P_m \times POP)/D_m$, when correlated with GRO-2:0. This variable has a simple r of only +.15. But when air service, colleges, manufacturing, population, and race are held constant, it goes to +.36. This is far above the 1 percent level (now $\pm.24$). It is also well above the equivalent partials for its elements: P_m reads +.21 under the same control set, POP is one of the variables held constant (equivalent to a .00 partial), and $1/D_m$ reads +.20.

Interpretation. Spillover growth theoretically should manifest itself in a gravity relationship.[7] But most of the gravity variable evidence denies the spillover hypothesis. With the over-10,000 sample, a gravity relationship cannot prevail in the Southwest in the face of predominantly slow growth among cities within 40 miles of an SMSA (table 10–1). Still, the over-5,000 sample gives the hypothesis some support. Given the conflicting findings, one can only say that the gravity evidence is inconclusive.

Assume, however, that the over-5,000 sample reaches the truth and that a gravity relationship between the SMSA and growth in its hinterland does exist in the Southwest. Is this a spillover relationship? Or is it more likely that subregional factors or compromise locations are responsible?

Spillover, as expounded in Berry's filter-down theory, is a dubious explanation. The original Hoover-Thompson filter-down theory sees new (innovating) industries becoming old and shifting from skill orientation to wage or market orientation; the result is either an urban-to-rural shift or geographic decentralization. It is not claimed that, where urban-to-rural shifting occurs, industry relocates near the original urban center. Indeed, Hoover and Thompson both use textiles as an example, and textiles shifted from the Northeast (not any one metropolitan area) to the Southeast. In the more common situation where an industry disperses nationally to move closer to its markets, the movement is again to new regions. Moreover, factories that go to nonmetropolitan cities go there directly; they do not require that intermediate plants first be established in nearby SMSAs. In other words, the Hoover-Thompson version of filter-down is a poor foundation for Berry to build on if he wants to argue that growth proceeds from metropolitan areas "outward to the intermetropolitan periphery."[8]

Berry substitutes the concept of innovation for the concept of new industry. The change is partly substantive: "innovation" downplays manufacturing technology and emphasizes the finished good and its adoption. Berry feels that innovations filter down through a metropolitan hierarchy and outward to smaller cities in the hinterland of each metropolis. This filtering is equated with growth. But Berry offers only one detailed example—television—to support his theory, and this example is unacceptable. In making the conceptual shift from production to product, he has lost the connection between employment or population growth and the spread of the innovation. Television's outward spread from metropolis to nearby cities did not bring "growth" as a "consequence." There was no spilling over of television manufacturing to nearby cities. Television stations did spread; but their employment effects are trivial, and most small cities do not even have stations. As for sales and service employment, that is essentially a redistribution of local employment, resulting from consumers spending their money on television instead of on something else; there is no net increase in spending or retail employment. Likewise, the spread of set ownership cannot be equated with growth.

The study findings, then, do not seem to be explained by spillover growth in the relatively literal sense of metropolitan growth that spreads to nearby places.

Yet the possibilities are good that metropolitan growth *influences* nearby places and in that sense spills over. The well-known locational attractions of metropolitan areas, which result largely from past metropolitan growth, probably do lead some firms to choose compromise locations close to the metropolis. Also, rapidly growing regional markets surely cause some firms to locate near the largest and fastest growing segment of the market—the metropolis—in situations where the metropolis actually is near the center of a plant's market region. The metropolis itself may be avoided because of high taxes, labor union activity, and the like or because a place intermediate between two or more SMSAs gives better market access. Or the countervailing pull of resources, such as petroleum for the manufacture of petrochemicals, may lead some firms to locate off center relative to their markets—even while favoring resource areas located fairly close to metropolitan markets.[9]

On the other hand, metropolitan growth might not even be an important influence. It could stem from the same factors that caused the hinterland to grow—and might even, to some extent, be caused by hinterland growth. The causal factors could include not only strong regional markets but an attractive climate and natural resources. The more remote cities could be outside the market, climate, or resource sphere of influence—for example, in hotter or more arid areas. This would explain the gravity relationship.

Notes

1. Edgar M. Hoover, *The Location of Economic Activity* (New York: McGraw-Hill, 1948), pp. 174–76, and *An Introduction to Regional Economics* (New York: Knopf, 1971), pp. 150–51; and Wilbur R. Thompson, "The Economic Base of Urban Problems," in Neil W. Chamberlain, ed., *Contemporary Economic Issues* (Homewood, Ill.: Irwin, 1969), pp. 6–9. Cf. David M. Smith, *Industrial Location* (New York: John Wiley & Sons, 1971), pp. 455–57.

2. Brian J.L. Berry, "Hierarchical Diffusion: The Basis of Developmental Filtering and Spread in a System of Growth Centers," in Niles M. Hansen, ed., *Growth Centers in Regional Economic Development* (New York: Free Press, 1972), pp. 108–36; and Berry, *Growth Centers in the American Urban System,* vol. 1 (Cambridge, Mass.: Ballinger, 1973), pp. 7–9, 63, 74–75.

3. Berry, "Hierarchical Diffusion," p. 136.

4. Ibid., p. 112.

5. See Leonard F. Wheat, *Regional Growth and Industrial Location: An Empirical Viewpoint* (Lexington, Mass.: D.C. Heath, 1973), pp. 6–20, 21, 183–89, 208–9.

6. See Robert M. Lichtenberg, *One-Tenth of a Nation* (Cambridge, Mass.: Harvard University Press, 1960), pp. 125–27, 131, 132–33; and Benjamin Chinitz and Raymond Vernon, "Changing Forces in Industrial Location," *Harvard Business Review* 38, no. 1 (January-February 1960): 126–36.

7. Cf. Berry, "Hierarchical Diffusion," pp. 113–17.

8. Ibid., p. 108. For a skeptical view, see Smith, *Industrial Location,* p. 456.

9. Cf. Glenn E. McLaughlin and Stefan Robock, *Why Industry Moves South* (Washington, D.C.: National Planning Association, 1949), p. 54: "In several cases, supply and cost of natural gas have led companies to choose places for market oriented plants which were somewhat removed from central distribution points."

11 Racial Mix

Variation among cities in their nonwhite population percentages is a promising factor for explaining growth. Several things might link fast growth with predominantly white populations. First, place discrimination in the South might cause firms seeking plant locations to avoid cities with heavily black labor forces. Second, black out-migration from the South could mean high out-migration rates for cities with high proportions of blacks. This effect might be reversed in Oklahoma and Texas, which have had considerable black in-migration too; but the inflow is to metropolitan areas, so we could still expect an outflow from small cities. Third, job discrimination combined with better education and skill levels for whites probably means that in-migration to nonmetropolitan cities with rising job opportunities is white. (This would be reverse causation: growth affecting racial mix.) Finally, racial mix might function as a proxy for colleges, since most students and faculty members are white.

Racial Mix Significance Tests

Census statistics do not include the black population percentage but do include what usually amounts to the same thing: the nonwhite population percentage. (The nonwhite segment will often be predominantly Mexican-American in Texas cities and might sometimes emphasize Indians in Oklahoma. However, since these groups also suffer from job discrimination, the factor being measured could be much the same.) The nonwhite percentage is the basic variable for racial mix. It is abbreviated RACE.

Chi-Square Tests. Table 11-1 compares the racial mix distributions of the fast and slow groups. This is another instance where the over-5,000 sample will be examined in addition to the over-10,000 sample. The over-5,000 sample, with its larger number of cases, offers some very high significance readings. These contradict some weak and probably misleading partial correlations from the over-10,000 sample.

Starting with the over-5,000 sample, we find a definite tendency toward slow growth in cities that are at least one-third nonwhite. A complementary tendency is for fast growth in cities that are less than one-fifth nonwhite. When the five intervals are reduced to two, with 33 percent and up as the highest interval, χ^2 is 5.26 for the Southeast—barely short of the 2 percent level. For the

Table 11-1

Frequency of Cases by Nonwhite Percentage (All States)

Percent Nonwhite	Southeast		Southwest		South	
	Fast	Slow	Fast	Slow	Fast	Slow
Over-5,000 Sample						
40% or more	7	15	9	10	16	25
33% to 39%	11	17	2	8	13	25
20% to 32%	19	18	17	21	36	39
10% to 19%	21	11	5	4	26	15
0% to 9%	12	9	27	17	39	26
Total Cities	70	70	60	60	130	130
Over-10,000 Sample						
40% or more	2	9	3	5	5	14
33% to 39%	4	5	2	5	6	10
20% to 32%	8	6	8	10	16	16
10% to 19%	11	4	3	1	14	5
0% to 9%	4	5	13	8	17	13
Total Cities	29	29	29	29	58	58

Southwest, a two-interval breakdown dividing at 20 percent is optimal. χ^2 is now 3.38, a little short of the 5 percent level. The same two-interval breakdown sends χ^2 to 8.44 for the overall South—comfortably above the 1 percent level.

The differences are sharper but, due to fewer cases, less significant with the over-10,000 sample. A three-interval breakdown, with 20 to 39 percent as the middle interval, tells that the Southeast differences are significant at the 5 percent level: χ^2 is 6.00. The Southwest differences are not significant. But for the overall South, a three-interval breakdown using 20 to 32 percent as the middle interval sends χ^2 to 8.26, above the 2 percent level.

Racial mix is really more significant than table 11-1 suggests. The table 11-1 findings are somewhat corrupted by generally low nonwhite percentages in the northern and western parts of the South—in Virginia, Kentucky, Tennessee, Oklahoma, and South and West Texas. In these states most cities are below 20 percent nonwhite, and quite a few are below 10 percent: the 33 percent and 20 percent norms for differentiating between fast and slow do not apply. This is why table 11-1 sometimes has greater fast-slow contrasts in the 10 to 19 percent interval than in the lowest interval, which is loaded with border-South cities.

Table 11-2 seeks to avoid this problem by dropping the troublesome states. The remaining states—the Carolinas, Georgia, Florida, Alabama, Mississippi, Arkansas, Louisiana, and East Texas—will be called the *Deep South*. Compare tables 11-1 and 11-2 under the "South" heading. Note that the Deep South's over-10,000 sample retains all cities at or above 33 percent nonwhite and twenty-eight out of thirty-two cities in the 20 to 32 percent interval but only seven of thirty cases below 10 percent.

Table 11–2
Frequency of Cases by Nonwhite Percentage (Deep South)

Percent Nonwhite	Southeast		Southwest		South	
	Fast	Slow	Fast	Slow	Fast	Slow
Over-5,000 Sample						
40% or more	7	14	9	10	16	24
33% to 39%	10	16	2	8	12	24
20% to 32%	16	14	17	19	33	33
10% to 19%	12	4	4	2	16	6
0% to 9%	3	0	8	1	11	1
Total Cities	48	48	40	40	88	88
Over-10,000 Sample						
40% or more	2	9	3	5	5	14
33% to 39%	4	5	2	5	6	10
20% to 32%	7	5	8	8	15	13
10% to 19%	5	1	2	0	7	1
0% to 9%	2	0	4	1	6	1
Total Cities	20	20	19	19	39	39

Now the fast-slow contrasts are vivid. The over-5,000 sample has about the same number of fast cities in the top two intervals as in the bottom two for the overall South. But there are forty-eight slow cities at or above 33 percent compared to seven below 20 percent. If a three-interval breakdown with 20 to 32 percent as the middle interval is used, χ^2 is 10.10 for the Southeast, 7.20 for the Southwest, and 17.02 for the overall South. The Southeast and South values top the 1 percent significance level, and the Southwest value reaches the 3 percent level.

The over-10,000 sample lacks enough cases in the two lowest intervals for a three-way breakdown to be used in computing χ^2 for the Southeast and Southwest; reduced significance is the result. Nevertheless, a two-interval breakdown using 33 percent and up as the highest interval provides a χ^2 of 4.90 for the Southeast, significant at about the 3 percent level. Under a three-interval breakdown for the South, χ^2 is 13.02, well above the 1 percent level.

Does using cutoffs below 20 percent allow racial mix to differentiate between fast and slow cities in the border states too? The answer is as follows:

Percent Nonwhite	Over 5,000		Over 10,000	
	Fast	Slow	Fast	Slow
20% and up	4	8	1	3
10–19%	10	9	7	4
0–9%	28	25	11	12

These breakdowns suggest that the 20 percent cutoff still applies outside the

Deep South. But relatively black (by state norms) cities less than 20 percent non-white do not suffer. In the over-5,000 sample, the two lowest intervals have virtually identical fast-slow ratios. The over-10,000 sample actually has faster growth in the 10 to 19 percent interval than in the lowest interval.

Correlation Tests. In the correlation tests, RACE was supplemented by three dummy variables inspired by the chi-square findings. These were RACE $\geq$ 33, RACE $\geq$ 20, and RACE $\geq$ 33:20. The first two are valued at one in cities equaling or exceeding the indicated nonwhite percentage and at zero elsewhere; RACE $\geq$ 33:20 is valued at two for cities at or above 33 percent; at one for cities in the 20–32 percent range, and at zero elsewhere.

Since the over-10,000 sample adequately describes the racial mix correlation findings, the discussion will focus on it. The highest simple r's came from the two dummies listed below. Three r's that are based on GRO-% instead of GRO-2:0 are marked with asterisks.

Variable	Southeast	Southwest	South
RACE $\geq$ 33	–.29	–.21*	–.25*
RACE $\geq$ 33:20	–.30*	–.26	–.27

All three columns have significant values. The –.30 reading for RACE $\geq$ 33:20, based as it is on the augmented sample (always used with GRO-%), is significant at the 1 percent level. The –.26 for the same variable in the Southwest reaches the 5 percent level. Both r's in the last column exceed the 1 percent level. Taken in conjunction with the chi-square findings, these r's provide convincing evidence of a genuine relationship between racial mix and growth.

The Deep South effect, discussed in connection with chi-square, can be partly controlled by holding constant some of the regional variables. The following partials hold constant COAST and ISOL for the Southeast; DELTA, W-TEX, and ISOL for the Southwest; and SE-SW, COAST, DELTA, W-TEX, and ISOL for the South. In each instance the best racial mix variable is RACE $\geq$ 33:20. The partial r's:

Variable	Southeast	Southwest	South
RACE $\geq$ 33:20	–.37	–.34	–.32

The Southeast and South partials reach the 1 percent level (well above for the South); the Southwest partial gets to the 2 percent level.

Another problem is that cities with high nonwhite percentages tend to have low wages. The low wages, which attract industry, partly offset the adverse effect of racial mix. If EARN (alone) is held constant, RACE $\geq$ 33:20 has these partials:

Variable	Southeast	Southwest	South
RACE ≥ 33:20	-.37	-.33	-.34

Once more the partials are significant at the 1 percent level for the Southeast and South and the 2 percent level for the Southwest.

If EARN *and* the previously named regional variables are controlled, even higher partials result. They are:

Variable	Southeast	Southwest	South
RACE ≥ 33:20	-.43	-.39	-.38

All three partials are safely above the 1 percent level.

When the standardized control sets are used, the best race variables are those ordinarily used in these sets (but excluded for these tests): RACE ≥ 33 for the Southeast, RACE ≥ 20 for the Southwest, and RACE ≥ 33:20 for the overall South. Their standardized partials are as follows:

Variable	Southeast	Southwest	South
RACE dummy	-.38	-.42	-.20

These partials are significant at the 1 percent level for the Southeast and Southwest and at the 5 percent level for the South. The findings, then, are consistent: growth is significantly lower where the nonwhite percentage is high.

Problems of Interpretation

The introduction to this chapter indicated that racial mix might represent (1) the avoidance of cities with proportionately high black populations by firms locating new plants, (2) high black out-migration from cities with high black percentages, (3) in-migration of whites to fast-growing cities, or (4) high white population percentages in college towns. Is it possible to clarify which relationship or relationships really exist?

Discrimination. This study provides no evidence one way or the other concerning whether industry is deliberately avoiding cities with high black percentages. However, it is possible to express an informed opinion on the matter. McLaughlin and Robock found in the late 1940s that discrimination was indeed important in southern plant location: "Because of company policy or as a concession to 'local custom,' none of the labor oriented plants surveyed [of over 20 such plants among 88 surveyed] employs Negroes. Consequently, in selecting a location, only the segment of the labor force which will be employed is considered by the company."[1]

By the 1960s, racial hiring practices had changed in the South. Discrimination was under widespread attack, and at least the national companies were getting away from the "local custom" approach to hiring in their southern plants. Yet the discrimination problem was hardly solved. Hansen, investigating southern counties that in the 1960s either reversed previous population declines or accelerated from relative stagnation, finds that industry was selecting counties with overwhelmingly white racial compositions. "These areas have one element of homogeneity that is even more striking than their industrial expansion: although they are southern they have proportionally fewer blacks than the nation as a whole."[2]

Hansen goes on to argue that even enlightened industrialists may have economically valid reasons for avoiding predominantly black areas: "Past and present discrimination against blacks in the provision of manpower services and health, education, and other human resource investments has created a labor force that may really be relatively less productive, and marginal firms in particular cannot afford experiments based on social concern."[3] In this regard, Hansen notes that most of the blacks displaced by agricultural technology in the South between 1950 and 1969 had less than four years of schooling.

Regardless of whether the underlying motive is racial or economic, place discrimination is almost certainly still present. And the relatively weak empirical support for the three alternative hypotheses, discussed next, makes discrimination look like the strongest factor underlying the significance of racial mix.

Outmigration. Recent decades have brought heavy black migration from the South to outside regions, as well as from rural to urban areas. Lansing and Mueller found that of a little under three hundred southern-born blacks interviewed in a 1962-63 survey, barely over one-fourth were still living in the labor market area where they were born.[4] Figures from the 1970 census show that 18 percent of the country's blacks over five years old migrated from the South to other regions.[5] A high nonwhite population percentage thus has obvious possibilities as an indicator of out-migration potential. On the other hand, agricultural mechanization was a major force behind the black migration: many of the migrants came from farms—as laborers, tenant farmers, and sharecroppers—rather than from towns. The question of whether racial mix influenced migration from cities is therefore still open.

The migration variables, not yet examined, provide some evidence bearing on this question. MIGR (1950–60 county net migration rate) and MIGR > 5 (a dummy identifying significantly positive net migration) are high where there is net in-migration and low where there is out-migration. We are looking for negative intercorrelations between RACE and MIGR: high nonwhite percentages associated with negative net migration.

The intercorrelations are surprisingly low. The highest r's are ones of -.18 in the Southeast (MIGR correlated with RACE $\geq$ 20), -.25 in the Southwest (MIGR $>$ 5 correlated with RACE $\geq$ 33:20), and -.15 for the South (MIGR correlated with RACE $\geq$ 33:20). These tests are crude, because 1950 instead of 1960 racial mix should be compared with 1950–60 migration: cause (race) should come before effect (migration). Still, 1960 racial mix should be a fairly good surrogate for 1950 mix, so the tests are not unreasonable. And what the tests seem to say is that migration is not significantly related to the racial mix of cities. Or, if we assume that the intercorrelations would have been a little higher had RACE used 1950 data, the intercorrelations would still appear to be too low to explain very much of the relationship between racial mix and growth.

This conclusion gets added strength from two other considerations: first, the lack of an agricultural displacement migration stimulus for urban blacks and, second, generally low mobility for blacks vis-à-vis whites. The mobility factor brings up our next hypothesis.

White Mobility. A third possibility is that racial mix is more an effect than a cause of growth. If the workers migrating to new jobs in fast-growing cities are mostly white, this will reduce the nonwhite population percentages in those cities. Are the in-migrants mostly white?

There is strong evidence that they are. For one thing, blacks are generally less educated than whites, and mobility rises with education—once we get outside the South-to-North black migration stream. Looking at the percentage of adult males aged twenty-five and up who migrated between March 1964 and March 1965, Lansing and Mueller found migration rates of 4.0 percent for those with eight years or less of schooling, 6.0 percent for those with four years of high school, and 8.8 percent for those with one or more years of college.[6] Beyond education, black mobility is weakened by occupational status, lack of financial reserves, and discrimination. Another Lansing and Mueller finding is that blacks had five-year mobility rates averaging 11 percent less than the average for the entire population even after education, occupation, and urbanization were controlled.[7]

It is less certain that white in-migration in fast-growing cities has much effect on the fast-slow racial mix differentials. The hypothesis that it does can be tested by comparing 1960 racial mix with both prior (1950–60) and subsequent (1960–70) percentage growth in population. If RACE has a higher correlation with G:50–60 than with GRO-%, this would suggest causation running from growth to racial mix. The augmented sample, which uses GRO-% and thereby provides a uniform basis of comparison, provides these r's between growth and whatever racial mix variables perform best:

Variable	Southeast	Southwest	South
G:50–60	–.18	–.06	–.09
GRO-% (1960–70)	–.30	–.21	–.25

The comparison shows that, in each region, racial mix is more closely related to subsequent than to prior growth. Chronology—1960–70 (GRO-%) coming after 1960 (RACE)—points to 1960–70 growth as the effect and 1960 racial mix as the cause. Beyond these findings, we have the pronounced fast-slow differences revealed in table 11–2 for cities that are one-third or more nonwhite. These differences certainly cannot be explained by in-migration. White mobility probably does make a small contribution to the generally low nonwhite percentages in fast-growing cities. But causation seems to run mainly from racial mix to growth.

White College Towns. A final possibility is that racial mix is a proxy for colleges: a low nonwhite percentage may represent a high percentage of white students and faculty members in the population.

This possibility is perfectly reasonable but is easily disproven. The intercorrelations between the racial mix and college variables are quite low. RACE $\geqslant$ 33 and COL-4 are the pair with the highest intercorrelation in each region. But the r's, though they have the expected sign, are low: –.17 for the Southeast, –.09 for the Southwest, and –.13 for the South.

Partial correlations with just the college variables from the standardized control sets held constant reiterate the unimportance of any proxy relationship. Holding colleges constant sends RACE $\geqslant$ 33 from a simple r of –.29 to a partial of –.24 in the Southeast, sends RACE $\geqslant$ 33:20 from –.26 to –.29 (an increase!) in the Southwest, and keeps RACE $\geqslant$ 33:20 at –.27 in the South.

The fact is that there are so many "white" towns without colleges that racial mix does not get much support from the college factor. Rather, the correlations between racial mix and growth seem to result primarily from discrimination, secondarily from black out-migration, and to a very limited extent from reverse causation, or the effect of growth—acting via white migration to growing cities—on racial mix.

Notes

1. Glenn E. McLaughlin and Stefan Robock, *Why Industry Moves South* (Washington, D.C.: National Planning Association, 1949), p. 69.

2. Niles M. Hansen, *The Future of Nonmetropolitan America* (Lexington, Mass.: D.C. Heath and Co., 1973), p. 164.

3. Ibid.

4. John B. Lansing and Eva Mueller, *The Geographic Mobility of Labor* (Ann Arbor: University of Michigan, Survey Research Center, 1967), p. 264.

5. Based on U.S. Bureau of the Census, *1960 Census of Population,* Series PC(2)-2D, "Lifetime and Recent Migration," table 9, p. 54.

6. Lansing and Mueller, *Mobility,* p. 43

7. Ibid., p. 50.

12 Urban Amenities

Industrial location literature retells with variations the story of the entrepreneur who locates his factory in the city that has his favorite golf course. This illustrates the role of personal considerations in industrial location. Many personal considerations can be subsumed under the heading "urban amenities." Industrialists are human beings and, like other humans, are interested in having a nice place in which to live.[1] (They also recognize that it is easier to attract managerial and professional talent to such places.) "Nice" refers to such things as an attractive business district and modern shopping centers, with stores and service enterprises of adequate size and variety; entertainment, recreational, and cultural facilities; pleasant residential areas with good housing; and health and medical services and facilities—things that are generally more prevalent in larger cities. Most urban amenities cannot be tested for significance, because adequate statistics are lacking. But three—housing, health services, and hospitals—offer possibilities.

Residential Areas

No really satisfactory variable is available for comparing residential neighborhoods and housing in different cities. But there is an outside possibility that the level of professional and technical employment is an adequate proxy: professional and technical employees have higher incomes and generally demand better housing. The relevant statistic is the 1960 census male employment figure for "professional, technical, and kindred workers," converted to a per-capita basis. PROF/P is the abbreviation.

Chi-Square Tests. PROF/P—the per-capita variable—is not available for chi-square purposes, but total professional, technical, and kindred employment is. The absolute figure, like total skilled worker employment, was eliminated from the correlation tests because of its proxy relationship to population. However, now that population has been found neutral in its relationship to growth, any positive relationship between professional employment and growth cannot be attributed to population.

Table 12-1 compares "professional, technical, and kindred" employment levels in the fast and slow cities. When all sample cities are included, the findings are strongly influenced by high professional employment levels in college towns.

Table 12-1

Frequency of Cases by Professional-Technical Employment

P-T Employment	Southeast		Southwest		South	
	Fast	*Slow*	*Fast*	*Slow*	*Fast*	*Slow*
All Cities						
1,000 or more	4	0	4	0	8	0
900 to 999	0	0	2	2	2	2
500 to 899	5	4	4	8	9	12
250 to 499	10	14	13	11	23	25
Under 250	10	11	6	8	16	19
Total Cities	29	29	29	29	58	58
Noncollege Cities						
1,000 or more	2	0	0	0	2	0
900 to 999	0	0	0	1	0	1
500 to 899	2	4	3	8	5	12
250 to 499	8	13	10	10	18	23
Under 250	10	11	5	8	15	19
Total Cities	22	28	18	27	40	55

To control the college effect, another comparison headed "noncollege" eliminates the college towns.

In the first comparison—"all cities"—there is not much difference between the two groups except at the upper extreme in employment. Both subregions have four cities with professional-technical employment of over 1,000; all eight cities are fast-growing. Eight is not enough for chi-square testing: at least ten in the top category (or at least five per cell) are needed. But when a two-interval breakdown dividing at 900 is used, the fast-slow difference for the South is significant at the 5 percent level: χ^2 is 4.56.

The implication that high professional employment stimulates growth is misleading, however. Six of the eight cities above 1,000 and nine of the twelve above 900 are college towns. Six of the nine college towns have major universities. Fast growth in college towns, not residential amenities, is what has been detected.

The second comparison removes the college factor. Now there are no significant differences between the fast and the slow cities. Chi-square testing, then, does not provide evidence that residential amenities—as estimated from professional employment—stimulate growth.

Correlation Tests. The simple correlations for PROF/P lean heavily on the college factor. The comparative simple correlation findings for PROF/P and COL-3 (used generically here to represent whatever college variable produces the particular *r* shown for a region) suggest this.

Variable	Southeast	Southwest	South
PROF/P	+.35	+.27	+.30
COL-3	+.35	+.37	+.36

Here PROF/P stays close to and generally a little below COL-3. PROF/P is significant at the 1 percent level for the Southeast and South and at the 5 percent level for the Southwest. If GRO-% is substituted as the dependent variable, PROF/P shows an exceptionally high r of +.41 for the Southeast—the highest simple r reached by any variable in the augmented (fast-moderate-slow) Southeast sample.

To get rid of the distortion caused by colleges, we can hold constant just the college variables from the standardized control sets. The results:

Variable	Southeast	Southwest	South
PROF/P	+.23	+.07	+.15

Now no r is significant, although the Southeast's +.23 partial comes close. But if we switch to GRO-% as the dependent variable and hold constant four regional variables in addition to the college variable, PROF/P goes to +.27 for the Southeast. This is barely short of the 1 percent level.

If PROF/P is a real influence but is too weak to register clearly in the presence of other influences, and if it is not heavily duplicated by other influences, it should show significant standardized partials. But, with GRO-2:0 as the dependent variable, the standardized partials are even lower than those just examined. They are:

Variable	Southeast	Southwest	South
PROF/P	+.15	−.18	+.03

Despite the insignificance of these partials, it is noteworthy that the Southeast's r remains well above zero. And when GRO-% replaces GRO-2:0 as the dependent variable, r becomes +.23 for the Southeast. This r is significant at the augmented sample's 5 percent level.

Interpretation. The consistently higher partials found for the Southeast are intriguing. Although insignificant when GRO-2:0 is the dependent variable, they are often quite significant with GRO-%. The question is: what do these significant partials represent?

An obvious possibility is that PROF/P actually is a proxy for residential amenities. This interpretation, of course, requires an explanation of why these amenities are significant only in the Southeast. Could the explanation have something to do with the rural orientation of southeastern industry? Rural communities are more apt to lack residential and other urban amenities, whereas the comparatively urban cities where industry locates in the Southwest might be relatively uniform in the amenities they offer. Shortcomings due to ruralness could be compounded by run-down conditions resulting from community age in the Southeast; southwestern cities are generally newer and more apt to have modern facilities. Lack of residential amenities could thus be a common problem in the Southeast but an exceptional one in the Southwest. If so, manufacturing has good reason to be more choosey in the Southeast when it comes to amenities.

Another possibility is that, even with college variables held constant, PROF/P is a proxy for a residual college influence. COL-3 and the other college variables are semidummies rather than continuous variables. They do not measure either student enrollment or faculty population. But PROF/P is probably somewhat proportional to these figures, which in turn might be better correlated with growth than is COL-3. But if PROF/P is a better measure of colleges, why the negative standardized partial for the Southwest?

In the final analysis, PROF/P's significant Southeast partials opposite GRO-% are ambiguous. They might or might not point to an urban amenities influence. They are encouraging enough, however, to suggest that further research using better measures would have a reasonably good chance of confirming that residential amenities affect community growth.

Health and Medical Services

Census employment figures for "medical and other health workers" are useful for gauging comparative levels of health and medical services. Separate figures are available for salaried and self-employed, male and female. A choice was necessary, because clerical constraints prevented the combining of categories. The self-employed male figure was used, because this category undoubtedly has most of the doctors. Putting this figure on a per-capita basis gives us the health-medical variable, MED/P.

Chi-Square Tests. MED/P is another of the variables that were used in absolute form for chi-square testing; the per-capita version was available only for correlation analysis. Table 12–2 compares total health-medical employment for the fast and slow cities. We are looking for higher health-medical employment levels in the fast cities. For reasons to be explained shortly, the table includes a subsidiary breakdown of cities below 15,000 population.

When all cities are included in the analysis, there are no significant differences between the fast and slow cities in either subregion or in the overall South. Nevertheless, the Southeast offers an interesting finding. Only 5 fast cities compared to 12 slow ones have less than twenty-five health and medical workers. Yet

Table 12-2
Frequency of Cases by Health-Medical Employment

	Southeast		Southwest		South	
H-M Employment	Fast	Slow	Fast	Slow	Fast	Slow
All Cities						
40 or more	9	9	13	12	22	21
25 to 39	15	8	8	8	23	16
Under 25	5	12	8	9	13	21
Total Cities	29	29	29	29	58	58
Below 15,000						
40 or more	0	0	1	2	1	2
21 to 39	11	5	3	4	14	9
Under 21	3	11	7	4	10	15
Total Cities	14	16	11	10	25	26

there are equal numbers of fast and slow cities with forty or more. This suggests that low medical service levels might inhibit growth in the smaller cities but not in the larger ones, possibly because the larger ones all have adequate service levels.

To check the small-city-only hypothesis, subsidiary tables covering only the cities below 25,000, below 20,000, and below 15,000 were prepared. Each reduction in the population ceiling sharpened the fast-slow disparity. The health-medical employment distributions for the cities below 15,000 population, where the disparity is greatest, appear in the lower half of table 12-2. The lowest interval has been reduced to twenty or less to provide maximum differentiation between the fast and slow cities. In the Southwest, the differences are of no consequence. But the Southeast now shows more than twice as many fast as slow cities with twenty-one or more health-medical workers. Among cities with twenty or less health-medical workers, we find 3 fast compared to 11 slow cities.

The Southeast differences are now significant at about the 3 percent level: χ^2 is 4.95.

Correlation Tests. MED/P was supplemented by a second variable, MED $\geqslant$ 25, in the correlation tests. MED $\geqslant$ 25 is a dummy valued at one in cities with at least twenty-five health and medical workers and at zero elsewhere. The simple correlations for these variables are as follows:

Variable	Southeast	Southwest	South
MED/P	+.02	−.10	−.04
MED $\geqslant$ 25	+.27	+.04	+.15

MED/P shows nothing of interest. But MED $\geqslant$ 25 has an *r* of +.27, significant at the 5 percent level, for the Southeast. This r is not supported by that of +.04 for the Southwest; and the +.15 figure for the South, though higher, is insignificant.

The standardized partial correlations give even less indication of a significant health-medical influence. They are:

Variable	Southeast	Southwest	South
MED/P	+.10	+.12	+.04
MED $\geqslant$ 25	+.14	+.01	+.08

All of these r's are far below their corresponding 5 percent significance levels.

Interpretation. The chi-square and simple correlation findings for the Southeast foster optimism about a possibly important discovery. But the optimism dims quickly. One problem is that the Southwest offers no similar findings and no reason for being different. For example, in the chi-square test of cities below 15,000 population, the Southwest cities with twenty or less health-medical workers are not generally closer to twenty than the Southeast cities. And, since distances to metropolitan areas run higher in the Southwest, one cannot argue that the Southwest cities can do without because of better access to metropolitan area health services.

Closer scrutiny of the Southeast findings reveals that 8 of the 14 Southeast cities below 15,000 and with twenty or less health-medical workers have nonwhite population percentages of 20 percent or more. Seven of these 8 relatively nonwhite cities have slow growth. It thus appears that racial differences between the fast and slow cities in the lowest interval may be largely responsible for the growth differences.

The conclusion emerges that health and medical services, as measured by MED/P, are not significantly related to growth. The qualification "as measured by MED/P" could be important, though. One wonders whether a simpler measure that counted only physicians might have been enlightening.

Hospitals

The adequacy of local hospitals was measured by hospital employment. Two hospital variables were used, HOSP (total hospital employment) and HOSP/P (hospital employment per capita). Absolute variables like HOSP are not ordinarily promising for correlation with relative variables like GRO-% and GRO-2:0. But with hospitals the absolute form of the variable is unusually inviting: the quality of hospital care and the range of services tend to be related to hospital size, and very small hospitals might be weaker magnets for industry than relatively large ones. HOSP gains further potential when one considers that the cities in

Table 12-3
Frequency of Cases by Hospital Employment

Hospital Employment	Southeast		Southwest		South	
	Fast	Slow	Fast	Slow	Fast	Slow
All Cities						
300 or more	5	6	4	5	9	11
200 to 299	5	1	3	3	8	4
100 to 199	11	13	8	12	19	25
50 to 99	8	6	8	6	16	12
Under 50	0	3	6	3	6	6
Total Cities	29	29	29	29	58	58
Below 15,000						
100 or more	7	8	1	4	8	12
50 to 99	7	5	5	3	12	8
Under 50	0	3	5	3	5	6
Total Cities	14	16	11	10	25	26

the over-10,000 sample all had at least twenty and generally had at least fifty hospital workers. That is, all apparently had hospitals; so the number, size, or quality of hospitals rather than have and have-not might be crucial.

Chi-Square Tests. Table 12-3 distributes the fast and slow cities according to their total hospital employment. (Again, the per-capita figure was not available for chi-square testing.) Another distribution in the lower half of the table covers just the cities below 15,000—cities where hospital facilities are most likely to be marginal.

The table gives no indication that hospitals are significantly related to growth. It is true that the Southeast puts in the slow column all three cities with less than fifty hospital employees. But with only three cases, this could easily be due to chance. Moreover, all three cities are 50 or more miles from air service; they have a handicap that heavily overshadows low hospital employment. Finally, the Southeast evidence is contradicted by the Southwest evidence, which shows twice as many *fast* cities in the same interval.

Because the findings obviously are statistically insignificant, χ^2 was not computed.

Correlation Tests. The simple correlations for HOSP and HOSP/P reflect the results of the chi-square analysis. They are:

Variable	Southeast	Southwest	South
HOSP	+.09	−.15	−.03
HOSP/P	+.08	−.24	−.04

Note that the r's for the Southwest and South even have the wrong sign. The -.24 for HOSP/P in the Southwest is not only negative but close to significance. This and the other negative r's are of course spurious in the sense that they cannot possibly mean that weak hospitals help growth. These r's evidently stem from a proxy connection between hospital employment and manufacturing: HOSP and HOSP/P have respectable Southwest intercorrelation of +.51 and +.50 with MFG > 0, which has a -.28 simple r in the Southwest. If MFG > 0 is held constant for the Southwest, HOSP and HOSP/P show partials of -.01 and -.12.

The following standardized partials continue to deny that hospitals influence growth:

Variable	Southeast	Southwest	South
HOSP	-.03	-.22	-.10
HOSP/P	+.02	-.28	-.06

All of these partials are negative—the wrong sign. Neither these nor any other partials obtainable with different control variables or by substituting GRO-% for GRO-2:0 give any indication of a significantly positive relationship between hospital employment and growth.

Interpretation. The evidence of chi-square, simple correlation, and partial correlation analysis is entirely contrary to the hypothesis that hospitals aid growth. However, deficiencies in the analysis make it advisable to remain open to the possibility of a hospital influence. The hospital variables used have severe limitations as measures of hospital quality. And, since all sample cities have hospitals— or at least enough hospital workers to staff a small hospital—we have not been able to assess the effect of having no hospital at all. Conceivably, those smaller cities that lack hospitals find it hard to attract industry.

Note

1. See Glenn E. McLaughlin and Stefan Robock, *Why Industry Moves South* (Washington, D.C.: National Planning Association, 1949), pp. 108-9. Also see David M. Smith, *Industrial Location* (New York: John Wiley & Sons, 1971), pp. 90-92, 145.

13 Economic Conditions

The local characteristics discussed in the preceding chapters all involved causal hypotheses. This chapter departs from causation to look at some noncausal hypotheses that stress prediction rather than explanation. Three factors—prior growth, prior net migration, and the unemployment rate—will be examined. All three describe local economic conditions; all three can reflect economic distress, even though slow growth and negative net migration can prevail in the face of relatively full employment. Economic conditions may be useful for predicting growth because they can represent hidden causal factors. Whatever causes fast growth, positive net migration, or full employment in one period will often have the same effect in the next period. The hidden factors for which economic conditions could be a proxy might well include some, such as natural resources, that are not covered in the preceding chapters. Economic conditions might also affect growth themselves, for example, by attracting new firms to expanding markets or by causing the out-migration of unemployed workers.

Prior Growth

For strictly a priori reasons, the most promising variable for predicting 1960–70 percentage growth in population would seem to be 1950–60 percentage growth: by using the same basic variable for two periods, we maximize the likelihood of a common relationship to the same causal factors. G:50–60 (1950–60 population growth rate) is therefore the first economic variable to be examined.

Chi-Square Tests. Table 13-1 compares the distributions of 1950–60 growth rates for the cities that were fast or slow by 1960–70 standards. Differences in state average 1950–60 growth rates interfere somewhat with initial comparisons: cities from fast-growing states can have regionally high growth rates yet really be slow relative to other cities from their states. For this reason, the table uses two bases of comparison. Under "Absolute Scale" at the top of the table, cities are grouped according to their actual 1950–60 growth rates. Under "Relative Scale" they are grouped according to the absolute percentage differences between their growth rates and their respective state median growth rates. The state medians are computed from the augmented sample.

In the Southeast, the contrast between fast and slow is not as great as one might expect. Under the absolute scale, the only eye-catching difference between

117

Table 13–1
Frequency of Cases by 1950–60 Population Growth Rate

1950–60 Growth	Southeast		Southwest		South	
	Fast	*Slow*	*Fast*	*Slow*	*Fast*	*Slow*
Absolute Scale						
40% or more	11	9	10	3	21	12
25% to 39%	7	4	7	5	14	9
10% to 24%	11	9	8	13	19	22
Under 10%	0	7	4	8	4	15
Total Cities	29	29	29	29	58	58
Relative Scale						
10%+ above median	13	9	10	5	23	14
3% to 9% above median	3	3	5	3	8	6
Within 2% of median	7	4	8	2	15	6
3% to 9% below median	5	4	3	5	8	9
10%– below median	1	9	3	14	4	23
Total Cities	29	29	29	29	58	58

the fast and slow cities is among cities that grew less than 10 percent between 1950 and 1960. Seven out of seven remained low for 1960–70. But seven is not enough cases for a chi-square test; and if the cutoff is moved up 2 percent to get at least ten cases (actually eleven) in the interval, there are three fast and eight slow cases. This is not a statistically significant difference. But under the relative scale, when the four highest intervals are merged to provide a two-interval break-down, χ^2 is 5.92. This is significant at the 2 percent level.

In the Southwest, the differences are greater. Under the absolute scale, a two-interval breakdown using a slightly different cutoff than any shown in the table provides maximum contrast:

1950–60 Growth Rate	Fast Cities	Slow Cities
30% and up	16	7
Below 30%	13	22

Here χ^2 is 4.60, significant at about the 4 percent level. Turning now to the relative scale, we find still greater contrast. When the three highest and the two lowest intervals are separately merged to form a two-interval breakdown, the lowest of the consolidated intervals has 6 fast but 19 slow cases. Now χ^2 is 10.12, significant far beyond the 1 percent level.

The South's breakdown allows complementary tendencies in the two sub-regions to reinforce each other. Highly significant differences result. Under the absolute scale, if the two highest intervals are merged to form a three-interval breakdown, χ^2 is 10.08. This exceeds the 1 percent level (9.21 for two degrees of freedom). Under the relative scale, a three-interval breakdown that merges the three highest intervals shown in the table works best. This time χ^2 is 19.00, far beyond the 1 percent level. The two-interval χ^2 is 13.22, equally significant.

Correlation Tests. The chi-square tests led to two supplemental variables for prior growth. These are G $\geqslant$ 25 and G $\geqslant$ 40:25, both dummies. The first is valued at one for cities where 1950–60 growth was 25 percent or more and at zero elsewhere; the second is the same except that it is valued at two where prior growth was 40 percent or more. G $\geqslant$ 25 had relatively low r's and will get no further consideration.

The simple correlations follow the chi-square pattern: low significance for the Southeast, high significance for the Southwest and overall South. Considering that G:50–60 is patterned after GRO-% (a continuous variable) rather than GRO-2:0 (a dummy), one expects higher correlations for G:50–60 when GRO-% is the dependent variable. But this is not the case: GRO-2:0 invariably does better (even when all regional variables are held constant). GRO-2:0 therefore remains the dependent variable for the r's that follow. Here are the simple r's:

Variable	Southeast	Southwest	South
G:50–60	+.18	+.34	+.26
G $\geqslant$ 40:25	+.14	+.34	+.23

The Southeast r's are not significant. But the +.34 readings for the Southwest and the +.26 for the South reach the 1 percent level.

An intriguing question is whether prior growth is significant as a proxy for factors already examined and represented in the standardized control sets. The following standardized partials provide insights:

Variable	Southeast	Southwest	South
G:50–60	+.10	+.39	+.25
G $\geqslant$ 40:25	−.03	+.36	+.18

The Southwest and South r's are still significant at the 1 percent level. This indicates that the corresponding simple r's did not depend to any great extent on proxy relationships. One-variable-held-constant tests with the standarized control variables give similar findings for the Southwest. The only variable that, held constant, causes an appreciable drop from the simple r for G:50–60 is MFG $>$ 0. Holding MFG $>$ 0 constant drives G:50–60 down to a partial of +.26. But the partial recovers and climbs above its original magnitude as other variables are controlled.

The Southeast's standardized partials are lower and more insignificant than the simple r's. Evidently the +.18 simple r for G:50–60 did rely somewhat on proxy factors. Be this as it may, the +.10 standardized partial is misleading in suggesting that prior growth cannot be used to predict subsequent growth in the

Southeast: some control combinations do render it significant. For example, G:50–60 is in the best six-variable multiple correlation set for the Southeast (table 14–1). If the other five variables in that set are controlled, G:50–60 goes to +.39, which is above the 1 percent level.

Interpretation. The comparatively weak relationship between prior and recent growth in the Southeast might seem surprising. But previous observations about Southeast-Southwest differences in the behavior of variables point to an explanation. The Southeast has relatively labor-intensive manufacturing. Because many new plants are seeking cheap labor, they tend to locate where labor market competition is weak—that is, where there is little other manufacturing. This tendency shows up in negative r's for E_m/E and MFG > 0. In this connection, we should remember that E_m/E is significantly negative only in the Southeast. Labor market competition is most likely to be weak where little or no prior growth has been experienced—where no other plant has recently come in and preempted the labor supply, or the cream of it. Therefore, we can surmise, places where 1950–60 growth was low had a consequent advantage for 1960–70.

Holding E_m/E—a measure of labor market competition—constant provides a simple test of the above explanation. This minimal control sends G:50–60 from its simple r of +.18 to a partial of +.25. Although +.25 is still a point below the 5 percent level, one more control variable does the trick: with both E_m/E and AIR $> 40:30$ held constant, G:50–60 reaches +.34. This test indicates that cities where prior growth was high do tend to grow faster in the Southeast if the offsetting effect of labor market competition is held constant.

In the Southwest, where industry is more capital-intensive, labor market competition has less influence on industrial location. Apparently for this reason, growth in one period has a much stronger relationship to growth in the next. The substance of this relationship is difficult to interpret. Among the factors represented in the Southwest's standardized control set, only air service (AIR > 25) and manufacturing (MFG > 0) allow G:50–60 to serve as a proxy for them: holding these two factors constant lowers r for G:50–60 a few points. However, the standardized partials have air service and manufacturing—along with several other factors—controlled. G:50–60 therefore must represent something else.

Conceivably, growth feeds on itself by creating markets and external economies that lead to further growth. But this is difficult to believe for cities that average around 20,000 in population, as the Southwest sample cities do: nonmetropolitan cities are generally too small to offer much in the way of markets or important external economies. A more promising conjecture is that G:50–60 is a proxy for different things in different cities—sometimes a fast-growing firm, sometimes a resource such as natural gas, sometimes a favorable market location at a point midway between two major metropolitan areas. Regarding resources, a high incidence of petroleum and natural gas deposits in the

Southwest might be a contributing factor in the Southeast-Southwest contrast in the behavior of G:50–60.

Prior Net Migration

The net migration rate (percentage in-migration less percentage out-migration) is an alternate measure of prior growth: growing places attract job seekers, who in turn contribute to growth. Net migration rates are not available for cities, so county figures were used—again for the 1950–60 period. The basic variable—the net migration rate—is labeled MIGR. In the Southeast, one finds a surprisingly low intercorrelation of +.11 between G:50–60 and MIGR; the Southwest shows a +.42 intercorrelation.The Southeast's low intercorrelation, as well as the Southeast-Southwest difference, may result from the use of county rather than city data for MIGR and from the Southeast's higher rural population density. Rural out-migration to metropolitan areas in other counties—sometimes in other states— probably offsets sample city growth to a considerable degree in the Southeast.

Chi-Square Tests. Table 13–2 compares the 1950–60 county net migration rates of the cities that grew fast with those that grew slowly in the subsequent decade. Note that most counties had negative net migration. This results from the inclusion in the county figures of rural population: rural people are migrating to metropolitan areas in other counties. A few positive migration rates in metropolitan areas cancel many negative ones for small, nonmetropolitan counties.

Since migration has some of the tendency that percentage growth has to

Table 13–2
Frequency of Cases by 1950–60 Net Migration Rate

1950–60 Migration	Southeast		Southwest		South	
	Fast	Slow	Fast	Slow	Fast	Slow
Absolute Scale						
+6% or more	6	2	7	0	13	2
–5% to +5%	6	6	5	6	11	12
–20% to –6%	13	18	9	15	22	33
–21% or less	4	3	8	8	12	11
Total Cities	29	29	29	29	58	58
Relative Scale						
3%+ above median	14	8	18	10	32	18
Within 2% of median	9	9	3	7	12	16
3%– below median	6	12	8	12	14	24
Total Cities	29	29	29	29	58	58

vary from state to state, a relative scale like that used in table 13-1 is shown along with the absolute scale. As before, the relative scale divides the cities into those with migration rates at least 3 percent (absolute) higher than the applicable state median, those that are close to the median, and those with rates at least 3 percent below the median.

The Southeast continues to show expected but insignificant tendencies toward faster growth among cities with high (positively inclined) prior net migration rates. Under the absolute scale, the fast-slow differences are minor: the most noteworthy finding is relatively fast growth among cities that had migration rates exceeding +5 percent. Under the relative scale, the differences are a bit sharper but still not close to significance.

The Southwest has a much stronger relationship between 1950–60 migration and 1960–70 growth; the prior migration findings agree with those for prior growth. Under the absolute scale, all seven cities with migration rates above 5 percent are fast-growing. Statistical significance is still lacking, though. Under the relative scale, the fast-slow contrast is greater. Now, when the two lower intervals are merged to get a two-interval breakdown, χ^2 is 3.38. This is still short of the 5 percent significance level (it reaches the 7 percent level), but it isn't far off.

The overall South, with its larger number of cases, provides very significant differences. Under the absolute scale, with the two lowest categories combined to provide a three-interval breakdown, the differences exceed the 1 percent significance level; χ^2 is 9.38. Under the relative scale, a two-interval breakdown— the two lowest intervals are merged—puts χ^2 at 5.94, or at about the 2 percent level.

Correlation Tests; A dummy variable, MIGR $>$ 5, was used to supplement MIGR in the correlation tests. It is valued at one for cities with net migration rates above +5 percent and at zero elsewhere.

The simple r's for migration are generally better when GRO-% is the dependent variable; hence, GRO-%'s r's are shown along with GRO-2:0's. MIGR $>$ 5, as the best-performing independent variable, represents migration. The simple r's:

Variable	Southeast	Southwest	South
MIGR $>$ 5 (GRO-2:0)	+.20	+.37	+.28
MIGR $>$ 5 (GRO-%)	+.30	+.31	+.30

All three r's obtained using GRO-% as the dependent variable are significant at the 1 percent level. The Southwest and South r's obtained with GRO-2:0 also reach the 1 percent level. The significant Southeast r, by the way, does not conflict with the chi-square finding of insignificant differences in the Southeast. That finding uses the regular fast-slow sample—the one used by GRO-2:0 for its insignificant *r*—whereas the +.30 Southeast partial uses the augmented (fast-moderate-slow) sample.

The partial correlations for migration are off sharply. MIGR > 5 generally provides the highest partials and is listed as the independent variable, although the Southeast partial opposite GRO-2:0 actually uses MIGR. The control sets used with GRO-% are similar but not identical to those for GRO-2:0. The standardized partials:

Variable	Southeast	Southwest	South
MIGR > 5 (GRO-2:0)	+.07	+.29	+.15
MIGR > 5 (GRO-%)	+.05	+.37	+.23

The Southeast *r*'s obviously are no longer significant; neither are the Southwest and South *r*'s opposite GRO-2:0. But opposite GRO-% the +.37 and +.23 readings for the Southwest and South still reach the 1 percent level.

What has happened in the Southeast? Migration, it seems, is a good proxy for colleges there, but not in the Southwest. The regular sample has a +.39 intercorrelation between MIGR > 5 and COL-3 in the Southeast; holding COL-3 constant sends MIGR > 5 from +.20 (simple *r*) to +.08 vis-à-vis GRO-2:0. With the augmented sample (GRO-%), MIGR > 5 moves from its simple *r* of +.30 to a partial of +.23 when four regional variables are controlled, then plummets to +.08 when COL-4 is also controlled.

Interpretation. The inability of past migration to predict future growth (apart from college-related growth) in the Southeast squares with the relative inability of past growth to do likewise. This duplication of findings reinforces the earlier inference that growth can be self-defeating in the Southeast: new labor-intensive plants preempt local labor supplies, thereby creating potentially competitive labor markets and deterring other labor-intensive plants from subsequently locating in the same cities. New plants in the Southwest are apt to be capital-intensive, having less impact on the labor market; and subsequent plants, also capital-intensive, are not particularly concerned about the labor markets anyway.

The Unemployment Rate

A third measure of economic conditions is the unemployment rate, or the percentage of the labor force that is unemployed. The basic variable, UNEMP, is the 1960 census unemployment rate. In theory, the unemployment rate should reflect prior growth: high unemployment can result if growth is too slow to absorb natural increases in the labor force. In actuality, the relationship is weak: G:50–60 and UNEMP have a –.19 intercorrelation in the Southeast and a +.22 intercorrelation—the wrong sign—in the Southwest. Out-migration of the unemployed from slow-growing places and frictional unemployment among in-migrants to fast-growing places may explain the weak relationship and the Southwest's positive sign. Unemployment, then, will not serve as an alternate measure of growth. Yet it may still be a good indicator of future growth. Cities with high unemployment are likely to experience out-migration—slow or negative growth—as the unemployed seek jobs elsewhere, and unemployment may be symptomatic of deficiencies in the wherewithall cities use to attract industry.

Chi-Square Tests. Table 13–3 compares the unemployment rate distributions for the fast and slow cities. In the lower half of the table, another relative comparison is made: cities are classified according to whether their unemployment rates are below, equal to, or higher than their respective state medians, which are derived from the augmented sample.

This time the more significant differences appear in the Southeast. Under the absolute scale, a progressively shifting fast-slow balance is seen in moving from the highest to the lowest unemployment interval. The lowest interval has all five of its cities placed in the fast column. If the two highest and two lowest intervals are separately merged to provide a three-interval breakdown, χ^2 is 8.00, significant at the 2 percent level. Under the relative scale, the three-interval breakdown shown in the table yields differences significant well beyond the 1 percent level: χ^2 is 14.12.

The Southwest has the expected differences, but they are insignificant. Perhaps the most distinctive feature of the Southwest's absolute scale distribution is its repetition of the 5–0 fast-slow split previously seen in the Southeast's lowest interval. The next two higher intervals offer a progressively shifting fast-slow balance, but the two highest intervals do not conform. Under the relative scale, potentially significant progressivity in the two lowest intervals is offset by the lack of any fast-slow difference among cities with the highest unemployment rates.

Turning to the overall South, we find the absolute scale distribution restoring the picture of a progressively shifting fast-slow balance: successively lower intervals put proportionately more cities in the fast group. The five-way unemployment breakdown shown in the table has fast-slow differences significant at the 1 percent level: χ^2 is 14.14, compared to a criterion figure of 13.28 for four degrees of freedom. A two-interval breakdown under the relative scale, with the two highest of the table's intervals treated as one, also has differences significant at the 1 percent level. Now χ^2 is 14.00, compared to a criterion figure of 6.64 for one degree of freedom.

Correlation Tests. Four dummy variables based on the chi-square findings were created to supplement UNEMP in the correlation tests. These are UNEMP $\geq$ 6, UNEMP $\geq$ 5, UNEMP $\geq$ 4, and UNEMP $\geq$ 5:4. The first three are 1–0 dummies;

Table 13-3
Frequency of Cases by 1960 Unemployment Rate

	Southeast		Southwest		South	
Unemployment	Fast	Slow	Fast	Slow	Fast	Slow
Absolute Scale						
8% or more	1	5	3	3	4	8
6% or 7%	7	12	9	11	16	23
5%	8	8	5	9	13	17
4%	8	4	7	6	15	10
3% or less	5	0	5	0	10	0
Total Cities	29	29	29	29	58	58
Relative Scale						
Above median	5	16	7	7	12	23
Same as median	4	7	6	13	10	20
Below median	20	6	16	9	36	15
Total Cities	29	29	29	29	58	58

UNEMP $\geqslant$ 5:4 is a 2-1-0 dummy derived by adding together UNEMP $\geqslant$ 5 and UNEMP $\geqslant$ 4.

With unemployment, the dependent variable giving the highest simple r's is always GRO-2:0. Three independent variables—UNEMP, UNEMP $\geqslant$ 4, and UNEMP $\geqslant$ 5:4—alternate in providing the highest r's:

Variable	Southeast	Southwest	South
UNEMP	-.43	-.13	-.27
UNEMP $\geqslant$ 4	-.31	-.31	-.31
UNEMP $\geqslant$ 5:4	-.38	-.30	-.34

The r of -.43 for UNEMP in the Southeast is nine points above the 1 percent significance level; that of -.31 for UNEMP $\geqslant$ 4 in the Southwest is significant at the 3 percent level; and that of -.34 for UNEMP $\geqslant$ 5:4 for the South is ten points above the 1 percent level. Unemployment is clearly a good indicator of future growth.

Before looking at the standardized partials for unemployment, we should view some one-variable-held-constant partials that control just the college variables from the standardized control sets. These partials indicate the extent to which low unemployment is a proxy for colleges: college towns, with their students and professors and general lack of industry, have low unemployment rates. The partials:

Variable	Southeast	Southwest	South
UNEMP	-.37	-.03	-.19
UNEMP $\geqslant$ 4	-.26	-.17	-.21
UNEMP $\geqslant$ 5:4	-.31	-.17	-.24

Despite a decline, the best r's for the Southeast and overall South are still significant at the 1 percent level. But those for the Southwest are no longer significant.

The standardized partials have about the same magnitude as the simple r's for the Southeast but are much lower (or of the wrong sign in one instance) for the Southwest. They are:

Variable	Southeast	Southwest	South
UNEMP	–.26	+.17	–.12
UNEMP ≥ 4	–.38	–.10	–.17
UNEMP ≥ 5:4	–.34	–.06	–.22

The best r's for the Southeast and South reach the 1 percent and 3 percent levels, respectively. But in the Southwest, very low r's—or the wrong sign—result from cumulative duplication of unemployment by most of the variables held constant. That is, the significant simple r's for the Southwest resulted from unemployment's ability to speak for other factors.

Interpretation. Why is high unemployment linked with subsequently low growth in the Southeast? Probably because places with high unemployment experience out-migration, and because those with low unemployment have in-migration. To judge from the fast growth of all ten cities with unemployment rates of 3 percent or less, the in-migration to healthy cities might be more important than out-migration from distressed areas. Unemployment might also represent hidden factors that influenced economic conditions in consecutive decades. But if proxy relationships were decisive, there should have been a significant relationship between 1950–60 growth and 1960–70 growth. None was found.

If out-migration of unemployed workers is a factor, why is UNEMP not related to growth in the Southwest too? As with other indicators showing Southeast-Southwest differences, the relatively capital-intensive nature of industry in the Southwest may provide the answer. Capital-intensive industry is more subject to cyclical fluctuations in unemployment; labor-intensive industry's unemployment is more frequently of the noncyclical variety. When unemployment rates fall, therefore, capital-intensive industry shows more recovery. This recovery can attract job seekers to affected cities, spurring population growth. If the unemployment rate fell between 1960 and 1970, southwestern cities with high 1960 unemployment would tend to show recovery-type growth. This would offset the migration effect found in the Southeast.

Did the unemployment rate fall? It did. The national unemployment rate went from 5.5 percent in 1960 to 4.9 percent in 1970.[1] The South's unemployment rate went from 5.5 percent[2] to 4.6 percent.[3] This drop might have dampened the out-migration of unemployed workers or at least produced subsequent countermigration in the Southwest's high-unemployment cities.

Notes

1. U.S. Bureau of the Census, *Statistical Abstract of the United States: 1971* (Washington, D.C.: 1971), table 327, p. 210.

2. The 5.5 percent is an adjusted figure based on a 5.6 percent figure for persons age fourteen and over published in U.S. Bureau of Labor Statistics, *Labor Force Unemployment in 1960,* Special Labor Force Report 14 (Washington, D.C.: 1961), table A2, p. A8. Since the comparable 1970 figure, as well as the national figure for 1960, is on an age-sixteen-and-over basis, and 0.1 adjustment has been estimated and made in the South's 1960 figure. This adjustment equals the difference between the original 5.6 percent age-fourteen-and-over national figure for 1960 and the revised 5.5 percent figure in the U.S. Bureau of the Census, *Statistical Abstract: 1971.*

3. *Statistical Abstract: 1971,* table 336, p. 215.

14 Multiple Correlations

Multiple correlation experiments followed the chi-square, simple correlation, and partial correlation tests. These final experiments look at the relationship—the multiple correlation, R—between the dependent variable (GRO-2:0) and a *group* of independent variables. By searching for the group that maximizes R, subject to limits on the number and significance of variables included, one can get a better idea of which variables are most important. The discussion covers the highest Rs obtained for two, three, four, five, six, eleven, and (overall South only) twelve significant variables; eleven and twelve are the most that can be used without including variables lacking significance at the 5 percent level. Some second-best ("alternate") combinations that give slightly lower Rs are also shown. This acknowledges other variables that do almost as well as those behind the best Rs. All Rs, whether best or second-best, are limited to variables significant at the 5 percent level. Most reach the 1 percent level.

Review: Independent Variables

Tables 14-1 through 14-6 summarize the multiple correlation findings. The variables in the tables were defined in detail in chapter 2 and again in the substantive chapters. However, definition recall and review of earlier substantive discussions will be facilitated if the variables are identified again. The following list does this.

Variable	Factor	Description
BUSNS, TRADE	Importance	Rand McNally business and trade ratings
MFG > 0, VA ⩾ 5	Mfg., negative side	Above-minimum MFG or value added (slow)
E_m/E	Mfg., negative side	Labor-intensive manufacturing (slow)
MFG, VA/P	Mfg., positive side	Capital-intensive manufacturing (fast)
AIR	Air service	Miles to nearest commercial airport
HWY	Highway service	Miles to nearest Interstate interchange
COL-3	Colleges	3-2-1-0 = Ph.D.-master's-bachelor's-none
SCHOOL	Lower education	Percentage of children (age 14–17) in school
D_m	SMSA proximity	Distance to nearest SMSA central city
$P_m G_m$	SMSA proximity	Population × growth rate, central city
TAX/P	Property taxes	Property taxes per capita, county
EARN	Wage level	Median annual earnings, operatives
SKIL/P	Wage level	Skilled workers per capita
RACE	Racial mix	Nonwhite population percentage

129

Variable	Factor	Description
G:50–60	Prior growth	1950–60 population growth rate
MIGR	Prior migration	1950–60 net migration rate, county
UNEMP	Unemployment rate	Percentage unemployed, 1960 census
ST-%P	Geographic location	State 1960–70 population growth rate
W-TEX	Geographic location	1-0 dummy: 1 = West Texas, 0 = all other
SE-SW	Geographic location	1-0 dummy: 1 = Southeast, 0 = Southwest

Omitted from the list are six local independent variables: POP (population), WATER (barge service), HI-SCH (lower education), PROF/P (residential amenities), MED/P (medical services, and HOSP/P (hospitals). These were not significant, except occasionally as proxies for something they were not intended to represent; neither did they enter the best multiple correlation sets. Also omitted are P_m, G_m, and some related gravity variables. These sometimes were significant but are not in the best R sets. State and regional variables not in the best R sets are likewise not on the list.

The variables listed (except MFG > 0, VA ≥ 5, and COL-3) are basic variables. This means they may take other forms, which are derived from the basic variables. For example, several dummy variables use 1-0 or 2-1-0 value structures to identify cities whose basic values are above, below, or between certain limits; MFG > 0 and VA ≥ 5 are examples. Mathematical transformations, such as 1/logHWY, are similarly derived. The Rs and associated partial r's in the tables do not necessarily come from the basic variables; many come from derived variables. Since correlations for a reciprocal are opposite in sign from those for the basic variable, all correlations for reciprocals (e.g., 1/HWY) are reversed in sign to agree with the basic variable's sign.

The Southeast

Systematic procedures compared essentially all possible sets (combinations) of significant variables. This identified the sets with the highest Rs. Tables 14–1 and 14–2 summarize the findings for the Southeast. Table 14–1 has the best sets for two, three, four, five, six, and eleven significant variables. Some second-best ("alternate") sets are also shown for two, three, and six variables so as to recognize variables that perform almost as well as those behind the best Rs. Three sets in which TAX/P and EARN, or else BUSNS and TRADE, are interchangeable give credit to both variables; the weaker of the pair is footnoted. At the bottom of each column, the R for that set appears. R has no sign; it may rest on a mix of negative and positive variables.

The best two-variable set consists of UNEMP and AIR $> 40:30$ (a 2-1-0 air service dummy). These two variables have the highest simple r's for all Southeast variables tested. Their R of .564 converts to an R^2 of .318. This means that

Table 14-1
Southeast: Best Multiple Correlation Combinations,
with Partial Correlations of Variables Used[a]

	Number of Variables in Combination								
Variable	Two	Alt. Two	Three	Alt Three	Four	Five	Six	Alt. Six	Eleven
BUSNS							+.55		
TRADE							$-.55^b$	-.31	-.34
MFG > 0									-.29
E_m/E							-.57	-.35	-.45
MFG							+.47		+.48
AIR	-.41		-.48	-.35	-.45	-.48	-.59	-.51	-.61
HWY		-.36		-.29	-.37	-.44		-.39	-.48
TAX/P			-.32		-.39	-.34		-.36	-.39
EARN			$-.31^b$		$-.36^b$	-.31			-.37
RACE									-.29
G:50-60							+.39		
UNEMP	-.42	-.41	-.47	-.40	-.46	-.51	-.53	-.40	-.38
ST-%P									-.33
Multiple R	.564	.538	.622	.614	.687	.722	.763	.740	.831

[a]Partials shown hold constant all variables listed in the same column except (1) the variable whose partial is shown and (2) any alternate variable footnoted with the letter b.
[b]EARN can replace TAX/P, or else TRADE can replace BUSNS, in this set. The alternate variable represents the same factor; either paired variable becomes very insignificant when the other joins the variables held constant.

together, they can statistically explain almost one-third (32 percent) of the fast-slow variation in growth.

The alternate two-variable set also uses UNEMP but substitutes 1/logHWY (0.8) for the air variable. The highway variable is a function of HWY, with 0.8 (or 1/log 16) being a constant value assigned to cities more than 16 miles from an Interstate System highway interchange.

Both three-variable sets build on the best two-variable sets. The best set adds TAX/P $\geqslant$ 40, a 1-0 property tax dummy, to the best two-variable set. Illustrating the overlap between taxes and wages, EARN (wages) can substitute for TAX/P $\geqslant$ 40 with hardly any change in R. (When TAX/P $\geqslant$ 40 is used, EARN's partial falls from -.31 to -.23.) The next-best set of three substitutes 1/log HWY (0.8) for the tax or wage variable. This substitution involves no duplication: the tax and wage partials actually climb.

The best four-variable set simply extends the best three-variable set. Once more the tax and wage variables are more or less interchangeable. Here and in other sets with interchangeable variables, the partial r's shown hold constant the better of the two interchangeable variables.

The best five-variable set modifies the air variable—it becomes AIR > 30— and brings in both the tax and the wage variable, instead of one or the other.

Because of duplication, TAX/P $\geq$ 40 and EARN have lower partials (indicating lower significance) here than in the previous set. Yet they remain significant, and this is important: both their significance and their joint participation in the best five-variable set show that taxes and wages have an appreciable degree of independence from each other.

The best six-variable set reverts to the best two-variable set, substitutes UNEMP $\geq$ 4 for UNEMP, and then builds in new directions. This time three manufacturing variables enter: $E_m/E \geq$ 25:20:15, MFG, and either BUSNS or TRADE. BUSNS and TRADE may have some nonmanufacturing substance but, when MFG > 0 is not held constant, serve mainly to identify nonmanufacturing cities; they substitute for MFG > 0. The relationship of BUSNS and TRADE to each other and to MFG > 0 is apparent from TRADE's decline from -.55 to -.24 and MFG > 0's decline from -.37 to -.13 when BUSNS enters the set last in a stepwise correlation series. Another of the new variables, E_m/E, stresses the amount rather than the presence or absence of manufacturing; its substance seems to combine wages (E_m/E has a +.50 intercorrelation with EARN), labor market competition, and the slow growth of labor-intensive industry. MFG depicts the positive side of manufacturing: fast growth in cities with high levels of capital-intensive industry. The sixth and least significant member of the set is G:50–60, the 1950–60 population growth rate.

The alternate six-variable set goes back to the five-variable set, substitutes 1/logHWY as the highway variable, substitues $E_m/E \geq$ 25:20:15 for EARN, and then adds TRADE as a sixth variable. Overlap between E_m/E and EARN means that substituting $E_m/E \geq$ 25:20:15 for EARN makes little change in the substance of the earlier set. TRADE can again be regarded as a manufacturing variable with strong labor market overtones: entering it last produces a 29-point shift in MFG > 0, which goes from -.17 to +.12.

Tables 14–1 and 14–2 both show the highest R that can be reached for the Southeast without using insignificant variables. Table 14–2 has more detail. It is structured according to stepwise correlations—one variable at a time entering the set. Column one numbers the steps. Column two identifies the variable entered at each step. The last two columns give R and R^2. Read as a percentage, R^2 (coefficient of multiple determination) tells what percentage of the variation in growth is statistically associated with—not necessarily caused by—variation in the independent variables used.

Columns three, four, and five do not relate to the stepwise format. Column three gives each variable's simple r (nothing held constant). Column four shows the partial r resulting when the variable is entered last—that is, when the other ten variables in the eleven-variable set are held constant. Column five compares the F values for the variables in the completed sets (not the incomplete sets preceding step eleven). The 1 and 5 percent significance levels (F values) when eleven variables (Southeast and Southwest) or twelve variables (South) are used with the present sample are as follows:

Table 14–2
Southeast: Best Multiple Correlation for Eleven Variables

Steps	Variable	Simple r	Partial r if entered last	F (signif.) if entered last	Step-wise R	Step-wise R²
1.	1/logHWY(0.8)	+.39	+.48	13.68	.387	.150
2.	AIR > 30	−.38	−.61	27.00	.496	.246
3.	TAX/P ⩾ 40	−.07	−.39	8.21	.573	.328
4.	UNEMP ⩾ 4	−.31	−.38	7.76	.647	.419
5.	TRADE	+.04	−.34	5.85	.686	.471
6.	E_m/E ⩾ 25:20:15	−.33	−.45	11.81	.727	.529
7.	MFG	+.11	+.48	13.91	.774	.599
8.	EARN	−.10	−.37	7.10	.787	.619
9.	RACE ⩾ 33	−.29	−.29	4.17	.795	.632
10.	ST-%P	.00	−.33	5.69	.813	.661
11.	MFG > 0	+.11	−.29	4.16	.831	.691

Level	Southeast	Southwest	South
5%	4.05	4.05	3.94
1%	7.21	7.21	6.89

The variables are shown entering in their natural order—the one with the highest *r* or partial *r* as of that step enters at each step—except that the variable that is least significant in the completed set is suppressed from entering until last. (MFG > 0's natural entry order is ninth.) Putting the least significant last lets the table show what *R* and R^2 would be if based on the ten strongest variables.

Eight of the variables in table 14–2 are in one or another of the preceding sets; only RACE ⩾ 33, ST-%P, and MFG > 0 are new.

RACE and ST-%P are complementary; each depends on the other for its significance. As explained before, ST-%P does not speak for itself when correlated with GRO-2:0: its "wrong sign" partial (−.33) is proof of this, and its .00 simple *r* further illustrates that geographic location per se cannot influence a city's status as fast or slow (2 or 0) when each state contributes as many fast as slow cities to the sample. What ST-%P does is compensate for the tendency of other factors to be, on balance, less stimulating in the fast-growing states or less inhibiting in the slow-growing ones. The slow ones are predominantly East Coast states, and COAST (the 1–0 East Coast dummy) can replace ST-%P with hardly any effect on *R,* which merely slips to .828. Primarily ST-%P compensates for geographic variation in the effect of racial mix. Thus RACE ⩾ 33 moves from an *F* of 1.28 to one of 4.17 (shown) if ST-%P enters last. Incidentally, this *F* becomes 6.82 if two regional variables—COAST and ISOL—replace the one, ST-%P.

The presence of both TRADE and MFG > 0 in the set shows that these two variables, though similar in substance, are not identical. If the other nine variables are held constant, their partials are -.54 for TRADE and -.52 for MFG > 0. (POP now reads -.06; TRADE and MFG > 0 clearly are not population proxies.) The reduced last-step partials point to duplication.

The Southwest

Tables 14-3 and 14-4 describe the best Rs for the Southwest. The best two-variable set, shown in the first column of table 14-3, uses MIGR > 5 (a 1-0 dummy) and $\sqrt{COL\text{-}3}$. Combined, they have an R of .538. The second-best, or alternate, two-variable combination keeps $\sqrt{COL\text{-}3}$ but uses a different measure of prior growth, G $\geqslant$ 40:25 (a 2-1-0 dummy based on G:50-60).

The best three-variable set begins with two variables whose significance is at first dimmed by mutual interference: a -.56 intercorrelation between VA $\geqslant$ 5 and AIR $> 40:25$ reveals that air service tends to stimulate growth where manu-

Table 14-3
**Southwest: Best Multiple Correlation Combinations,
with Partial Correlations of Variables Used**[a]

			Number of Variables in Combination						
Variable	Two	Alt. Two	Three	Alt. Three	Four	Five	Six	Alt. Six	Eleven
MFG > 0									-.50
VA $\geqslant$ 5			-.50		-.49	-.43	-.48	-.43	— [b]
AIR			-.49	-.37	-.56	-.58	-.57	-.54	-.64
HWY									-.33
COL-3	+.42	+.43						+.30	
SCHOOL									+.41
D_m			-.45	-.45	-.50	-.50	-.58	-.45	-.44
P_mG_m									+.42
TAX/P				-.48	-.46	-.44	-.46	-.42	-.49
EARN						-.35			— [c]
SKIL/P									-.35
RACE									-.43
G:50-60	— [d]	+.41				+.28		+.30	+.48
MIGR	+.43								
W-TEX							+.32		+.29
Multiple R	.538	.527	.623	.608	.721	.747	.773	.770	.844

[a]Partials shown hold constant all variables listed in the same column except the variable whose partial is shown.
[b]VA $\geqslant$ 5 is replaced by its equivalent, MFG $\geqslant$ 0, in this set.
[c]EARN is replaced by its equivalent, SKIL/P, in this set.
[d]G:50-60 is replaced by its equivalent, MIGR, in this set.

facturing inhibits it, and vice versa. If VA $\geqslant$ 5 is entered first, AIR $\geqslant$ 40:25 goes from a simple r of -.17 to a partial of -.41, entering second. The third variable is $D_m > 160$, a 1-0 dummy identifying cities more than 160 miles from a major metropolitan area. In the alternate three-variable set, TAX/P $\geqslant$ 40 replaces (but does not duplicate) VA $\geqslant$ 5.

The four-variable set is simply the best three-variable set with TAX/P $\geqslant$ 40 added; it is the best and alternate three-variable sets combined. In this and all but one of the subsequent sets, the air variable becomes the most significant member—the one with the highest partial. The best five-variable set is another extension. It just adds G:50-60 to the previous set.

The best six-variable set goes back to the four-variable set, changes the tax variable to TAX/P, and then adds EARN $\geqslant$ 3000 and W-TEX. The wage variable's ability to join TAX/P without losing significance shows that wages has some independent significance in the Southwest; it is not purely a proxy for taxes. W-TEX, whose positive sign means that it assigns additional growth to West Texas cities, compensates for the tendency of other variables to overpenalize West Texas. In particular, $D_m > 160$ underestimates for West Texas: W-TEX moves from an insignificant F value of 0.01 to a significant F of 5.77 if $D_m > 160$ is entered last in a stepwise correlation series.

The second-best six-variable set is essentially the best five-variable set with $\sqrt{COL-3}$ added. The only other change is the substitution of G $\geqslant$ 40:25 for G:50-60: the 2-1-0 growth dummy replaces the basic variable.

Table 14-4 provides supplementary detail on the best eleven-variable set, also found in table 14-3. Eleven is still the most variables that can be used while excluding insignificant ones. As in table 14-2, all variables but the last have been entered in their natural stepwise correlation order; the last, W-TEX, would have entered sixth if not suppressed. Entering W-TEX last allows us to see what R and

Table 14-4
Southwest: Best Multiple Correlation for Eleven Variables

Steps	Variable	Simple r	Partial r if entered last	F (signif.) if entered last	Stepwise R	Stepwise R^2
1.	$D_m > 160$	-.37	-.44	11.31	.365	.133
2.	G:50-60	+.34	+.48	13.95	.474	.225
3.	AIR > 25	-.17	-.64	32.95	.562	.316
4.	MFG > 0	-.28	-.50	15.04	.662	.438
5.	TAX/P	-.27	-.49	14.45	.709	.503
6.	P_mG_m	+.09	+.42	10.01	.733	.537
7.	RACE $\geqslant$ 20	-.24	-.43	10.66	.751	.564
8.	SCHOOL	+.01	+.41	9.57	.788	.621
9.	HWY > 8	-.00	-.33	5.55	.810	.656
10.	SKIL/P	-.21	-.35	6.54	.828	.686
11.	W-TEX	.00	+.29	4.35	.844	.712

R^2 are when based on the best ten variables in the set. W-TEX, incidentally, again modifies the effect of other variables rather than speaking for itself—just as it does in the best six-variable set and as ST-%P does in the Southeast's best eleven-variable set.

In table 14–4, MFG $>$ 0 is a replacement for VA $\geqslant$ 5 (manufacturing), and SKIL/P is a substitute for EARN $\geqslant$ 3000 (wages). The only substantively new variables are thus the ones entering at steps six through nine. Two of the new variables, RACE $\geqslant$ 20 and HWY $>$ 8, describe factors (racial mix and highways) represented in the Southeast. The only completely new variables in the R context, then, are $P_m G_m$ and SCHOOL. $P_m G_m$ is related to $D_m >$ 160 as a metropolitan area proximity variable. SCHOOL, as said before, seems to describe not education but the urban orientation of Southwest industry.

The South

Tables 14–5 and 14–6 cover the best Rs for the overall South. The best two-variable set combines the Southeast's strongest "economic conditions" factor (unemployment) with the Southwest's (prior growth): the variables are UNEMP $\geqslant$ 5:4 and G:50–60. The second-best set uses $\sqrt{\text{COL-3}}$ in place of UNEMP $\geqslant$ 5:4. Substantively, this is not much of a change, since unemployment and colleges are linked by the low unemployment in college towns.

The best three-variable set builds on the best two-variable set by adding AIR $>$ 40:25. The alternate three-variable set imitates the Southwest's best three-variable set, using the same three factors. This time the variables are AIR $>$ 40:30, VA $\geqslant$ 5, and SW $\times$ $D_m >$ 160. The last variable, remember, uses a dummy multiplier, SW (1 = Southwest, 0 = Southeast), to "zero out" the Southeast cities, where metropolitan area closeness is not positively related to growth.

The best four-variable set extends the best three-variable set by adding VA $\geqslant$ 5. Overlap between VA $\geqslant$ 5, a Southwest variable, and $E_m/E \geqslant$ 25:20:15, significant in the Southeast, deserves comment. The E_m/E dummy's partial declines from -.27 to -.10 when VA $\geqslant$ 5 enters last in stepwise correlations. Thus, in the context of the overall South, VA $\geqslant$ 5 obviously picks up much of what E_m/E measured earlier.

The best five-variable set is still another extension of the preceding one. Competing for the role of fifth variable are SW $\times$ $D_m >$ 160, with a partial of -.30, TAX/P, at -.29; and EARN $\geqslant$ 3¼:3, at -.28. SW $\times$ $D_m >$ 160 wins.

The best six-variable set again builds on the preceding one, except that $D_m >$ 160 now replaces SW $\times$ $D_m >$ 160. The sixth variable is TAX/P $\geqslant$ 40. It describes both taxes and wages: EARN $\geqslant$ 3¼:3 falls from -.26 (step five) to -.18 when TAX/P $\geqslant$ 40 enters the set.

The alternate six-variable set is a different extension of the best five-variable set. Going back to SW $\times$ $D_m >$ 160 as the "metro" variable, it uses 1/logHWY

Table 14–5
South: Best Multiple Correlation Combinations, with Partial Correlations of Variables Used[a]

Variable	Two	Alt. Two	Three	Alt. Three	Four	Five	Six	Alt. Six	Eleven	Twelve
VA ⩾ 5				−.40	−.32	−.36	−.36	−.38	−.41	−.31
E_m/E										−.25
VA/P									+.26	+.34
AIR			−.35	−.46	−.45	−.49	−.53	−.49	−.51	−.49
HWY								−.24	−.33	−.31
COL-3		+.37								
D_m				−.36		−.30	−.31	−.31	−.29	−.32
TAX/P							−.30		−.30	−.32
EARN							−.26[b]		−.30	−.25
G:50–60	+.31	+.30	+.39		+.37	+.36	+.36	+.37	+.29	+.31
UNEMP	−.38		−.37		−.36	−.32	−.35	−.34	−.44	−.46
SE-SE									−.32	−.25
W-TEX									+.25	+.29
Multiple R	.445	.438	.543	.534	.605	.650	.685	.675	.759	.775

[a]Partials shown hold constant all variables listed in the same column except (1) the variable whose partial is shown and (2) the footnoted variable (EARN) in the six-variable combination.

[b]EARN can replace TAX/P in this set with only a slight reduction in R. In this context, either variable can describe the joint effect of wages and taxes.

(0.8) as variable number six. This is the highway variable used earlier in most of the Southeast sets. It is also the next variable to enter if the best six-variable set is extended to seven steps, in which case R becomes .707.

Eleven variables is no longer the limit, but table 14–5 nevertheless includes an eleven-variable set for comparison with its Southeast and Southwest counterparts. This set begins with the best five-variable set. It then adds EARN ⩾ 3¼:3, VA/P, TAX/P, W-TEX, SE-SW, and SE/HWY. Most of these are from earlier sets. But VA/P and SE/HWY are new. VA/P (value added per capita) represents the positive side of manufacturing—fast growth in cities with high levels of capital-intensive industry. Its position in this set is equivalent to that of MFG in the Southeast's best eleven-variable set. SE/HWY (an abbreviated way of writing SE-SW × 1/HWY) is the highway reciprocal multiplied by the Southeast-Southwest dummy to "zero out" the Southwest cities.

Twelve is now the most variables that can be used without including ones that lack significance at the 5 percent level. Table 14–6 provides detail for the best twelve-variable set. The variables are shown entering in their natural order, except that the least significant is again entered last. This last variable—E_m/E ⩾ 25:20:15—is the only one not in the eleven-variable set; the twelve-variable set simply adds this variable to the preceding one. Three effects require comment.

Table 14-6
South: Best Multiple Correlation for Twelve Variables

Steps	Variable	Simple r	Partial r if entered last	F (signif.) if entered last	Step-wise R	Step-wise R^2
1.	UNEMP ⩾ 5:4	−.34	−.46	26.97	.337	.114
2.	G:50–60	+.26	+.31	11.21	.445	.198
3.	AIR > 40:25	−.28	−.49	33.25	.543	.295
4.	VA ⩾ 5	−.17	−.31	11.08	.605	.366
5.	SW × D_m > 160	−.25	−.32	12.02	.650	.423
6.	EARN ⩾ 3¼:3	−.19	−.25	6.67	.680	.462
7.	VA/P	−.03	+.34	13.16	.695	.483
8.	TAX/P	−.17	−.32	12.06	.705	.497
9.	W-TEX	.00	+.29	9.32	.719	.517
10.	SE/HWY	+.19	+.31	10.75	.726	.527
11.	SE-SW	.00	−.25	6.97	.759	.576
12.	E_m/E ⩾ 25:20:15	−.21	−.25	6.60	.775	.601

First, EARN falls from a partial of −.30 to one of −.25. This confirms that E_m/E (labor-intensive manufacturing) reflects wages to some extent. Second, VA ⩾ 5 falls from −.41 to −.31. This shows that E_m/E can pick up some of the magnetism of nonmanufacturing cities, which is what VA ⩾ 5 describes. Third, VA/P (capital-intensive manufacturing) goes up from +.26 to +.34. This shows that the positive side of manufacturing remains partly obscured until both negative facets are held constant.

The only previously significant factors not visible in table 14-6 are schooling, colleges, and racial mix. SCHOOL lacks significance for the overall South because its negative r for the Southeast cancels its positive r for the Southwest. COL-3 is the victim of cumulative duplication by other variables. Most important in this respect are UNEMP ⩾ 5:4 and E_m/E ⩾ 25:20:15—unemployment and the manufacturing employment percentage. RACE also suffers from cumulative duplication. Then too, the Deep South effect requires better control of regional differences than SE-SW and W-TEX provide. Things improve if COAST and ISOL are added to the set for better regional control while UNEMP ⩾ 5:4, E_m/E ⩾ 25:20:15, and G:50–60 are deleted to curtail the duplication. The result is a partial of +.30 for $\sqrt{COL-3}$ and one of −.25 for RACE ⩾ 33. Both r's exceed the 1 percent level. All factors found significant in earlier chi-square and correlation tests, schooling excepted, thus remain significant in the context of the South's best and most comprehensive R set, somewhat modified for two of the factors.

15 Recapitulation and Assessment

Chapter 14 completes the presentation of findings for the growth indicators—actual and potential—covered in the study. Now let us review the findings, attempting to assess the relative importance of the indicators. The findings involve chi-square, simple correlations, standardized partial correlations, a variety of other partials seen in multiple correlation contexts, and varying frequencies of representation of different variables in the multiple correlations. These findings will be summarized in three tables—one for the Southeast, one for the Southwest, and one for the overall South. Then a factor-rating system will be formulated and used to compare the various indicators.

Summary Tables

Tables 15-1, 15-2, and 15-3 summarize the test results for the Southeast, Southwest, and overall South, respectively. Capsule definitions and descriptions of the variables summarized—HI-SCH, P_m, and G_m excepted—appear at the beginning of chapter 14. HI-SCH is the percentage of high school graduates among people over twenty-five; P_m is the "metro" population, referring to the nearest SMSA's central city; and G_m is the 1960–70 "metro" growth rate.

As in tables 14-1, 14-3, and 14-5, the variables listed are basic variables; the only exceptions are MFG > 0, VA ≥ 5, and COL-3. But the statistics do not necessarily come from the basic variables. Derived variables—dummies, square roots, and other mathematical transformations—provide the figures whenever this gives more significant results. As before, correlations for reciprocals are reversed in sign to agree with the basic variable's sign. Similarly, because BUSNS and TRADE are shown on the same line but are opposite in sign, all correlations for BUSNS are reversed in sign to agree with those for TRADE, generally the stronger of these near-twin variables.

The chi-square results are always for whatever distributional breakdown gave the most significant findings. Thus, some chi-squares use a three-interval breakdown (two degrees of freedom) for the independent variable while others use a two-interval breakdown (one degree of freedom). Since the 5 and 1 percent significant levels are higher for two degrees of freedom than for one, degrees of freedom is indicated with asterisks in the chi-square column. The notation "n.s." in the same column means that chi-square was obviously not significant and was not computed.

A few correlations, though none of the standardized ones, use GRO-% rather than GRO-2:0 as the dependent variable. GRO-% provides a better fit, meaning an appreciably more significant r, in these instances.

The "Region-Constant Partial" column holds two to five regional variables constant: COAST and ISOL for the Southeast; DELTA, W-TEX, and ISOL for the Southwest; and SE-SW, COAST, DELTA, W-TEX, and ISOL for the overall South. Where GRO-% is the dependent variable, ST-%P and ST-%M are also controlled for this partial r. These partials compensate for geographic inconsistency in the relationships between some factors and growth. When GRO-2:0 is the dependent variable, in which case the regional variables always have simple r's of .00, the region-constant partials can only increase—never decrease—the magnitude of r; the regional variables offset overestimation or underestimation in certain states by the variables whose partial is shown. Region-constant partials using GRO-% additionally allow the regional variables to nullify the effect of state growth rates on city growth rates, so in this case the partials are sometimes lower than the simple r's.

The "Highest R Set Partial" heading refers to the multiple correlation sets in tables 14-1 to 14-6. These tables include "partial r if entered last" columns. If a variable is in more than one such set, the present tables use the r from the set where the variable had its highest partial.

"No. of R Sets Used in" is a count of the number of multiple correlation sets in tables 14-1 to 14-6 that included the basic variable or one derived from it. If a variable is in both the best and the second-best set for a given number of variables, only one appearance counts.

Table 15-1 summarizes the Southeast findings. Air service, the unemployment rate, and Interstate System highways stand out as the best indicators of growth potential. Chi-square is highest for unemployment, with highways second and air service farther back. Unemployment is highest in the simple r column, with air service second, colleges third, highways fourth. The standardized partials place highways .02 ahead of air service; unemployment is far behind. Air service leads among the highest R set partials, standing well ahead of the other two. Unemployment, air service, and highways are each in six multiple correlation sets—more than credited to any other variable.

Table 15-2 covers the Southwest findings. Now the strongest factors are metropolitan area distance, air service, property taxes, prior growth, and colleges. Prior growth, taxes, and colleges rank one, two, three in the chi-square column. The college factor leads among the simple r's, with taxes, metropolitan area distance, and migration (a close relative of prior growth) tied for second. Air service is a strong first under the standardized partials, with metropolitan distance second and taxes third. Air service and distance are again first and second under the R set partials; the other factors lag well behind. Air service, metropolitan distance, and taxes—along with the negative side of manufacturing—are in more R sets (five) than any other variable; prior growth is right behind.

Table 15-1
Southeast: Chi-Square and Correlation Summary

Basic Variable	Chi-Square	Correlations				No. of R Sets Used in
		Simple	Region-Constant Partial	Standard-ized Partial	Highest R Set Partial	
BUSNS, TRADE	n.s.	+.04	+.04	−.39	−.55	2
MFG > 0, VA ⩾ 5, and E_m/E	3.95*	−.33	−.33	−.39	−.57	2
MFG, VA/P	n.s.	+.11	+.11	+.34	+.48	2
AIR	7.46*	−.41	−.43	−.55	−.61	6
HWY	9.98*	−.39	−.41	−.57	−.48	6
COL-3	8.48*[a]	+.40[b]	+.41[b]	+.35		0
HI-SCH	4.44*	+.32[b]	+.34[b]	+.16		0
SCHOOL	7.04*	−.38	−.40	−.13		0
EARN	2.70*	−.14	−.15	−.35	−.37	4
TAX/P	n.s.	−.07	−.08	−.44	−.39	5
D_m	n.s.	+.01	+.08	+.27		0
$P_m, G_m, P_m G_m$	n.s.	+.15	+.20	+.17		0
RACE	4.90*[c]	−.30[b]	−.37	−.38	−.29	1
G:50–60	5.92*	+.18	+.19	+.10	+.39	1
MIGR	n.s.	+.30[b]	+.23[b]	+.07		0
UNEMP	14.12**	−.43	−.44	−.38	−.53	6

*Has one degree of freedom.
**Has two degrees of freedom.
[a]Based on over-5,000 sample to get adequate number of college cases.
[b]Based on GRO-% instead of GRO-2:0 as the dependent variable.
[c]Based on special Deep South breakdown.

Table 15–3 summarizes the results obtained by combining the Southeast and Southwest samples. Unemployment, prior growth, and air service stand out as the best indicators. Unemployment and prior growth are virtually tied for the highest chi-square, with colleges close behind. The college factor has the best simple r; unemployment is second and migration (related to prior growth) third. Air service has the best standardized partial; two also-rans—taxes and highways—rank second and third. Air service and unemployment rank first and second for the R set partials. Unemployment and prior growth are in the most R sets (seven), followed by air service (six).

Factor Scoring

One can see that the findings are not wholly consistent—not among regions and not among different criteria. If the many factors tested are to be evaluated objectively, some method of rating them is needed. A 100-point rating system

Table 15-2
Southwest: Chi-Square and Correlation Summary

		Correlations				
Variable	Chi-Square	Simple	Region-Constant Partial	Standard-ized Partial	Highest R Set Partial	No. of R Sets Used in
BUSNS, TRADE	n.s.	-.06	-.07	-.36		0
MFG > 0,						
VA $\geqslant$ 5	4.41*	-.28	-.33	-.45	-.50	5
MFG, VA/P	n.s.	-.07	-.08	+.08		0
AIR	n.s.	-.17	-.18	-.53	-.64	5
HWY	n.s.	-.00	-.00	-.33	-.33	1
COL-3	6.34*	+.43[a]	+.42[a]	+.14	+.43	2
HI-SCH	n.s.	+.31	+.34	+.08		0
SCHOOL	n.s.	+.01	-.01	+.36	+.41	1
EARN, SKIL/P	5.01*	-.29	-.30	-.34	-.35	2
TAX/P	9.40**	-.37	-.40	-.45	-.49	5
D_m	4.04*	-.37	-.43	-.47	-.58	5
$P_m, G_m, P_m G_m$	n.s.	+.18[a]	+.14[a]	+.40	+.42	1
RACE	n.s.	-.26	-.34	-.42	-.43	1
G:50-60	10.12*	+.34	+.37	+.39	+.48	4
MIGR	3.38*	+.37	+.39	+.29	+.43	1
UNEMP	n.s.	-.31	-.32	-.10		0

*Has one degree of freedom.
**Has two degrees of freedom.
[a]Based on GRO-% instead of GRO-2:0 as the dependent variable.

was therefore devised. It uses five criteria: chi-square, region-constant partial, standardized partial, highest R-set partial, and the number of R sets a variable is used in. A factor can earn up to six points per criterion per region, except that as many as nine (Southeast and Southwest) or ten (South) go with the last criterion. The theoretical maximum is thus 33 for the Southeast, 33 for the Southwest, and 34 for the South.

The second criterion, region-constant partial, can be viewed as a substitute for the simple r. In most cases, this partial and the simple r are identical or almost identical. But sometimes, most notably in the case of racial mix, regional variations in a factor's average value or in its impact make the simple r an unrealistic measure. Holding regional variables constant then provides a fairer appraisal of the factor's significance. Like the simple r, the region-constant partial does not prevent whatever distortions result from overlap between the factor being tested and other local factors.

The first four criteria—chi-square and the three correlations—award points on the basis of rank and significance, as follows:

Highest (or most significant) value 6

Second-highest (second most significant) value   4 or 5

Table 15–3
South: Chi-Square and Correlation Summary

Variable	Chi-Square	Simple	Region-Constant Partial	Standardized Partial	Highest R Set Partial	No. of R Sets Used in
			Correlations			
BUSNS, TRADE	n.s.	−.01	−.01	−.17		0
MFG > 0, VA ⩾ 5, and E$_m$/E	6.75**	−.21	−.24	−.27	−.41	6
MFG, VA/P	n.s.	−.03	−.03	+.18	+.34	2
AIR	7.39*	−.28	−.29	−.44	−.53	6
HWY	5.32*	−.22	−.28	−.37	−.33	3
COL-3	12.62*	+.42[a]	+.42[a]	+.27	+.37	1
HI-SCH	12.32**	+.30	+.30	+.08		0
SCHOOL	n.s.	−.22	−.23	+.10		0
EARN, SKIL/P	6.01*	−.21	−.23	−.25	−.30	3
TAX/P	8.24*	−.21	−.24	−.39	−.32	3
D$_m$	n.s.	−.25	−.30	−.31	−.36	5
P$_m$, G$_m$, P$_m$G$_m$	n.s.	+.12[a]	+.18[a]	+.08		0
RACE	13.02**[b]	−.27	−.32	−.20		0
G:50–60	19.00**	+.26	+.28	+.25	+.39	7
MIGR	9.38**	+.30	+.31	+.15		0
UNEMP	14.00*	−.34	−.36	−.22	−.46	7

*Has one degree of freedom. **Has two degrees of freedom.
[a]Based on GRO-% instead of GRO-2:0 as the dependent variable.
[b]Based on special Deep South breakdown.

Third-highest (third most significant) value 3

Other value significant at 1 percent level 2

Other value significant at 5 percent level 1

The second-highest value is scored at 5 rather than 4 when a correlation is within .01 of the highest and at least .02 above the third-highest; there are two such cases. Factors tied for a rank get full credit for that rank.

The last criterion, number of R sets used in, awards points according to the counts shown in the last column of tables 15-1, 15-2, and 15-3, except that (1) representation in the best or alternate two-variable set counts triple and (2) representation in the best or alternate three-variable set counts double. The multiple counting recognizes that it takes a stronger variable to enter the smallest combinations. Note, however, that no bonus results from being in the best *and* the alternate set for a fixed number of variables.

Table 15-4 presents the factor scores derived from this system. The factors are ranked by total score and, where two factors are tied, by number of regions giving the factor a score of two or better. Eight factors stand well ahead of the rest: (1) air service, (2) unemployment, (3) prior growth, (4) property taxes,

Table 15-4

Comparative Scores for Factors Related to Growth

Rank	Factor	Southeast	Southwest	South	Total Score
1.	Air Service	26	18	23	67
2.	Unemployment Rate	25	1	25	51
3.	Prior Growth	4	18	22	44
4.	Property Taxes	11	18	13	42
5.	Mfg. Negative Side	10	14	15	39
6.	Interstate Hwy. System	24	3	11	38
7.	Colleges	7	14	16	37
8.	Distance to Major SMSA	0	21	12	33
9.	Wages	8	7	9	24
10.	Racial Mix	7	7	6	20
11.	Prior Migration	0	8	4	12
12.	High School Percentage	3	2	4	9
13.	Mfg. Positive Side	5	0	4	9
14.	Percentage in School	4	4	0	8
15.	Business and Trade	7	1	0	8
16.	SMSA Population & Growth	0	5	0	5

(5) the negative side of manufacturing, (6) Interstate System highways, (7) colleges, and (8) distance to nearest major SMSA. Air service, with a 67 to 51 lead over unemployment, is far enough ahead to justify fairly high confidence that it is the best indicator of growth potential. No other factor has at least 18—or even 12—points in all three regions. However, the college factor has been weakened in the standings through duplication by unemployment in many of the best R sets. Without the unemployment variable, colleges conceivably would have replaced air service as the top-ranked factor.

In any case, colleges is probably a stronger determinant—contrasted with indicator—than unemployment. Colleges would at least rank second if unemployment per se could be divorced from the college element. Indeed, if we acknowledge that unemployment probably reflects other growth determinants besides colleges, it almost certainly belongs behind colleges where causation is concerned. This does not deny a deterministic element in unemployment: unemployed workers tend to migrate, causing population loss.

Prior growth, property taxes, the negative side of manufacturing, highways, and colleges are within seven points of one another. A slightly modified scoring system could easily alter their ranks. But if we again think in terms of causation, colleges and highways are probably the most important. The effect of colleges on growth is obvious. Highways theoretically could be a proxy for something else but has no apparent proxy relationships. The other three factors do. Property taxes seems to be largely a proxy for wages in the Southeast and gets some support from wages in the Southwest and South. The negative side of manufacturing, though partly a matter of slow growth in labor-intensive industries, also has a proxy relationship to wages: manufacturing cities have more competitive labor markets, which represent potentially if not actually high wages. Prior growth is a proxy for many factors that influence growth in consecutive periods.

Among the remaining factors, wages and racial mix might well belong nearer the top. The wage variables are too crude to capture the full significance of wages, and duplication by property taxes is a further obstacle to accurate estimation. The significance of racial mix is hard to measure because of geographic variation in the nonwhite population percentage: cities that are relatively high for their states may be absolutely low by regional norms. This and possible regional variations in discrimination patterns result in the Deep South effect, discussed earlier.

16 Conclusions

The importance ratings just presented and the interpretations from earlier chapters support a series of conclusions. These concern the usefulness and causal implications of the indicators. Additional conclusions, this time at a more general level, explain a logically consistent pattern of Southeast-Southwest differences in the strength of certain indicators.

The Indicators: Utility and Causation

The scores in table 15–4 say nothing about causation; they simply indicate which factors are relatively more useful than others for predicting fast and slow growth. The next task is to judge what conclusions are warranted about the relationship of each factor to growth. Is it causal? Is the indicator a proxy, or partly a proxy, for something else? Is there reverse causation—growth influencing the factor? What else might make either the relationship or the factor's score misleading? The following conclusions deal with these questions, taking each factor in chapter order.

Size and Importance. Population size does not affect growth in cities of 5,000 to 50,000 population. A special substudy does show somewhat faster growth for cities above 30,000. However, this advantage seems to depend on a higher incidence of colleges and air service among the larger cities; in any case, it is not statistically significant. The substudy also shows insignificantly faster growth among the smallest cities, particularly southeastern cities of 5,000 to 10,000 population. This fast growth below 10,000 might reflect the appeal of low wages for the Southeast's relatively labor-intensive manufacturing. And, in both the Southeast and the Southwest, it is related to the attraction of noncompetitive labor markets in places with little or no manufacturing. A statistical factor also contributes to slow growth rates among the smaller cities: population is the growth rate base, so low population makes it easier to show high percentage growth.

This brings up a related point. If non-SMSA cities above 5,000 have, ceteris paribus, about the same growth rates, it follows that absolute growth tends to increase with size. For example, a 10 percent growth rate means absolute growth of 1,000 for a city of 10,000 but of 3,500 for a city of 35,000. Although their growth rates are generally no higher, larger cities therefore have an advantage

147

where growth center policy is concerned. A growth center can be defined in this context as a place with relatively high potential for creating new jobs for people in the surrounding hinterland. If two or more cities serve the same hinterland, the one that can provide the most new jobs is in that respect best suited for development as a growth center. And the larger city is likely to provide more new jobs.

Business and trade importance are related to growth as proxies for manufacturing and might have independent significance in the Southeast. Partial correlation tests sometimes give business and trade a significant relationship to growth in the Southeast: the unimportant cities tend to grow faster. Usually, though, business and trade are insignificant when manufacturing is held constant. If the southeastern relationship is genuinely significant, the probable explanation is noncompetitive labor markets in the unimportant cities. This explanation is consistent with many other findings suggesting that much of the Southeast's industry prefers cities where wages or wage pressures are low.

Manufacturing. Existing manufacturing can have favorable or unfavorable effects on growth. The negative side of manufacturing itself has two facets, so in a sense there are three effects. On the positive side, cities with high levels of capital-intensive industry tend to grow fast. The variables VA/P (value added per capita) and MFG (Rand McNally manufacturing rating) reveal this tendency. It is significant only in the Southeast. And it is seen only when other variables, describing the negative side of manufacturing, are controlled; otherwise the positive variables lose their selectivity and describe manufacturing in general—relatively neutral. A causal relationship apparently exists. Because capital-intensive industry tends to be fast-growing, cities with this type of industry are apt to benefit from the growth of existing firms. Capital-intensive firms hire comparatively few workers, hence are less likely to bid up wages and repel new firms. On the contrary, new capital-intensive plants may even seek the skilled labor found where other capital-intensive plants are established.

On the negative side, labor-intensive manufacturing tends to have slow growth. E_m/E (manufacturing employment as a percentage of total employment) emphasizes this type of industry. In the Southeast, where industry is relatively labor-intensive and the effect in question is statistically significant, cities where E_m/E was 10 percent or less in 1960 all grew fast (six cases). Where E_m/E was above 20 or, especially, 25 percent, slow growth was the rule. The relationship hinges partly on the ability of low E_m/E to identify college towns. But a weaker relationship remaining when colleges are held constant looks causal. If a city's industry grows slowly, as labor-intensive industry often does, the city itself is likely to. Also, high levels of manufacturing employment threaten new firms with wage competition and recruitment problems. This discourages new industry.

Manufacturing's other negative effect applies to both the Southeast and the Southwest. This effect relates not to the amount of manufacturing but to its presence or absence. "Nonmanufacturing" cities, in the sense of cities with so little manufacturing that it is not an important economic activity, tend to grow fast; "manufacturing" cities—places where manufacturing is at least the leading secondary activity—tend to grow slowly, subject to the reservation that enough industry of the right kind can still produce fast growth. The apparent reason for slow growth in the manufacturing cities is that new plants prefer places where they can "cream" the labor supply, avoid wage competition, and perhaps influence community affairs. Opposition by existing firms (fearful of wage pressures) to community promotion in manufacturing cities could also be a factor.

Transportation. Good transportation can stimulate growth. In fact, proximity to a commercial airport—one with certificated airline service—is the best single indicator of growth potential for the South. The air stimulus is strong in both subregions but in the Southwest is initially obscured by the coincidence of significant amounts of manufacturing (unfavorable) with airline status (favorable). To benefit, a city need not have its own airport; it can be served by a nearby one. A nearby airport helps most if it is within 25 or 30 miles—roughly a half hour's drive. (Other research, but not the present study, indicates that the air stimulus is extra strong for cities within 10 or 15 miles of an airport.) However, cities within 40 miles of air service have some advantage, and findings for the over-5,000 sample in the Southwest suggest a weak stimulus from air service for cities as far away as 50 miles. The relationship of air service to growth is primarily causal. Firms locate close to air service to facilitate contact with customers, suppliers, and (in the case of branch plants) company headquarters. Businessmen consider both surface transportation and long drives to airports unsatisfactory alternatives for long trips.

Interstate System highways are a strong stimulus to growth in the Southeast—perhaps stronger than any other stimulus—but mean very little in the Southwest. Southeastern cities that are no more than 5 to 8 miles from the nearest interchange are the chief beneficiaries. The highway-growth relationship is definitely causal. The Interstate network was designed to connect major metropolitan areas, and neither past nor projected future growth rates for intervening small cities influenced highway routings; growth did not cause the highways. Rather, new manufacturing locates on the Interstate System in order to provide better service (time savings) to customers and to reduce the cost of shipping goods to market. Interstate highways have more impact in the Southeast because of its higher population density and hilly terrain. The resulting congestion, grades (a problem for trucks), and curves (passing and speed problems) impede traffic on regular highways, giving Interstate highways a bigger advantage.

Water transportation (barge service) is not a stimulus to growth. Indeed, the water transport variable even yielded correlations of the wrong sign. The wrong-sign correlations evidently reflect the decline of many of the old river cities, especially along the Mississippi River. Water transportation is no longer as important as it once was, and some cities whose existence was largely based on it are struggling to survive. Today the nation's inland and intracoastal waterways are used mainly to transport a limited number of bulk commodities and raw materials. Relatively few industries use the raw materials; and even these industries are generally more concerned with transporting finished goods, for which the slowness of barge transportation militates against its use.

Education. Higher and lower education are significantly related to growth. Colleges are especially important. The presence of a college or university is in one sense the best indicator of rapid future growth. Where they exist, colleges virtually guarantee fast growth, particularly in the case of advanced-degree schools (see table 7-1). Colleges were probably short-changed in the scoring because of two things: duplication by other factors (unemployment in particular) and the small number of college towns. With so few college towns, the college factor has less effect on region-wide variations in growth than it has in individual cases. The effect, of course, results from climbing enrollments and from resulting growth in college, retail, and service employment. However, the 1960–70 period may be misleading. The Vietnam war and population factors seem to have produced abnormally rapid enrollment increases, especially in graduate schools. College-related growth is now slowing down, making colleges a less reliable growth indicator for the present era.

A high-school-educated labor force, on the other hand, does not stimulate growth. The local population's percentage of high school graduates *is* a good indicator of growth potential, but mainly as a proxy for colleges. An unusually high percentage of high school graduates is likely to signify the presence of a college—the real stimulus. But when colleges are controlled, the high school percentage is not significantly correlated with growth. The high school percentage theoretically could also describe prior growth; migration of the better educated workers to growing places (jobs) could mean reverse causation. However, the high school percentage apparently eschews this role. One finds almost no intercorrelation between prior growth and the high school percentage, and holding prior growth constant does not appreciably affect the partial r's for the high school variable.

Another aspect of lower education offers more likelihood of a causal relationship. A high percentage of children in school signals slow growth in the Southeast but fast growth in the Southwest. Southeastern industry is comparatively labor-intensive and often seeks rural areas, where labor is cheap yet abundant—and less educated. Schooling becomes a proxy for rural orientation. Southwestern industry is less attracted to cheap labor and faces low population density—inadequate labor supplies—in rural areas. Also, the Southwest's higher proportion of capital-intensive manufacturing should mean higher demand for skilled workers. The need for adequate supplies of labor—particularly skilled labor—leads the Southwest's industry to relatively urban locations, where schooling is coincidentally higher. Some reverse causation is probably involved also: the better educated workers, whose children remain in school longer, migrate to fast-growing places, raising the average level of schooling.

Wages and Taxes. The next two factors—wages and taxes—can be treated jointly because (1) both are cost items for manufacturing, hence can deter new industry, and (2) they tend to be high or low in the same places, which makes it hard to separate their effects. Wage and tax level differences among states favor the use of relative indicators. Slow growth is typical in cities where median earnings for "operatives and kindred workers" are $200 or more above the median for all nonmetropolitan cities in the state. Fast, moderate, or slow growth is likely according to whether county property taxes per capita are $3 or more above, within $2 of, or $3 or more below the state median.

Although proxy characteristics cloud its interpretation, the wage factor looks like a good indicator for the Southeast. One interpretive problem is the high intercorrelation between wages and taxes (+.49 for the South). TAX/P often, though not always, has stronger partial correlations than EARN in the Southeast. But the findings of other studies concerning the importance of wages as a location factor in the Southeast justify allocating most of the wage-tax effect in the Southeast to wages. Another problem is that high wages go with relatively high employment in manufacturing (E_m/E); EARN and E_m/E have a +.50 intercorrelation for the Southeast. This means that sluggishness due to slow-growing, labor-intensive manufacturing might be mistaken for the effect of high wages. Still, some if not most of the adverse effects of high manufacturing employment result from the wage pressures of competitive labor markets. Thus wages and manufacturing are to some extent the same in substance.

In the Southwest, the joint effect of wages and taxes seems mostly attributable to taxes. TAX/P gives consistently higher correlations—simple and partial— than EARN in the Southwest. Also, the Southwest's industry is more capital-intensive and therefore more motivated to avoid high taxes on plant and equipment. Sometimes, though, neither wages nor taxes lies behind the relationship between high taxes and slow growth. Petroleum resources, and possibly other resources as well, inflate revenues in some Southwest cities. And because cities with resource economies tend to grow slowly, these revenues create the illusion of a tax effect. In short, being a good indicator may not imply that taxes per se are a major influence.

Metropolitan Area Proximity. "Filter-down" theories assume that the distance to and size and growth rates of major metropolitan areas affect the growth of surrounding smaller cities. In the Southeast, though, proximity to major metropolitan areas seems unrelated to growth. A minor exception, which involves too few cases for significance, is that six of seven cities in the over-10,000 sample that are over 200 miles from a metropolis of 250,000 or more have slow growth.

The Southwest, in contrast, shows rather consistent evidence of proximity relationships. Here the over-10,000 sample suggests a critical distance of 160 miles; beyond this slow growth sets in. The over-5,000 sample points to 80 miles as a critical distance. In addition, hinterland cities in the Southwest tend to grow fast if the nearest metropolis is relatively large or fast-growing. This tendency becomes quite significant when the metropolitan area's population is weighted by its growth rate. The over-10,000 sample does not show evidence of a gravity relationship—that is, of interaction between metropolitan "mass" (size, growth) and distance as they relate to nonmetropolitan city growth. But the over-5,000 sample provides some evidence—partial correlations—of a gravity relationship.

The observed proximity relationships are probably not causal in the sense of metropolitan growth spilling over into surrounding areas and attenuating with distance. Causal theories are weak and sometimes inconsistent with the concept of intraregional filtering. Filtering in a looser sense is more plausible: well-known metropolitan area attractions might lead some firms to adopt compromise locations, near enough to the metropolis to enjoy limited benefits but far enough away to avoid high wages and the like. Still more plausible is common causation. Regional stimuli such as markets and resources might be causing the fast growth of both (1) the largest and fastest growing metropolitan areas—which in fact happen to be Houston and Dallas–Ft. Worth—and (2) their closest hinterland cities. Regional liabilities, such as topography (Appalachia) and low rainfall (West Texas), might also operate: they might inhibit the most remote cities but not the metropolitan areas. Reverse causation, with resources operating through the hinterland cities to affect growth in the metropolitan areas, is yet another possibility; consider petroleum's role in the Southwest.

Race and Amenities. Two other factors—racial mix and urban amenities—are related in that both involve matters that, despite economic overtones, are heavily concerned with personal attitudes. Racial mix is a relatively weak but still useful indicator of growth potential. Cities with high nonwhite population percentages have generally slow growth. Race would be a much stronger indicator were it not for differences between Deep South and Border South states. Even so, special chi-square tests for the Deep South leave no doubt as to the significance of race. Cities that are one-third or more black tend toward slow growth; those that are one-fifth to one-third black have no tendency; and those that are under one-fifth black tend to grow fast. Several things contribute to this relationship. Discrimination is the most important: some firms avoid relatively black communities. Black out-migration from the South to other regions also affects growth in these cities. And there is some reverse causation: growing places attract whites, who lower the nonwhite percentages.

The urban amenities tested were residential neighborhoods, health and medical services, and hospitals. These are suspected of influencing the willingness of businessmen to live in certain places, hence to locate plants there. Unfortunately, the variables used for testing the amenity hypotheses were unsatisfactory (although causal inferences might have been possible after further analysis if significant relationships had materialized). Residential amenities did give tentative evidence of significance in the Southeast, but the evidence was weak and ambiguous. All one can say with certainty is that, as measured in this study, urban amenities are not useful growth indicators.

Economic Conditions. Three economic measures—prior growth, prior net migration, and unemployment—are among the leading indicators. Growth in the preceding decade is, for the Southwest, an outstanding indicator. In the Southeast, prior growth is a less effective indicator yet is significant. Both subregions give low growth potential to cities whose previous-decade populaton growth was below 10 percent. But only the Southwest shows proportionality between prior and future growth among cities with prior growth above 10 percent. Here prior growth of around 25 to 30 percent makes fast growth probable for the future. (The cutoff level could be expected to vary somewhat with secular change in the regional growth rate.) Prior growth of 40 percent or more is very auspicious. The connection between prior and future growth is essentially noncausal: prior growth is a proxy for other factors that stimulate growth in both periods.

Like prior growth, net migration in the preceding decade is a weak indicator for the Southeast but a good one for the Southwest. Cities with positive net migration of 6 percent or more are likely to grow fast; those with negative migration rates of at least 6 percent are likely to grow slowly; rates of +6 to –6 percent entail uncertainty. Intended as an alternate measure of prior growth, prior migration has only a +.11 intercorrelation with prior growth in the Southeast and— still lower than expected—a +.42 intercorrelation in the Southwest. This is why the two are treated as separate factors. But they do overlap, and both are proxies for other factors. The weakness of migration as an indicator in the Southeast arises partly from the use of county rather than city migration data. Southeastern counties have comparatively high rural populations, and rural out-migration to outside metropolitan areas overshadows urban in-migration (if any) when county figures are used.

The unemployment rate at the beginning of the growth period is an excellent indicator of growth potential in the Southeast: high unemployment signals low growth potential. In the Southwest, unemployment is a significant factor but less important. For 1960–70, all Southeast and Southwest cities with 1960 unemployment rates under 4 percent had fast growth. Growth potential for cities at or above 4 percent could be evaluated according to whether a city's unemployment rate was lower than, equal to, or higher than the state median for cities of 10,000 to 50,000. Unemployment's connection with growth is partly causal: out-migration of unemployed workers undermines growth, and in-migration to places with low unemployment bolsters growth. Unemployment can also be a proxy for other factors—most notably colleges—that influence growth. But despite its value as an indicator for 1960–70, unemployment might not predict well—especially outside of the Southeast—for a period witnessing a strong economic recovery.

Southeast-Southwest Differences

Many indicators are much more or less significant in the Southeast than in the Southwest; some are significant in just one subregion. Why? As pointed out earlier, the Southeast has generally lower wages than any other region. And it has high rural population density—which means that ample labor supplies exist in comparatively rural locations, where wages are lowest. Consequently, a disproportionate share of all labor-intensive industry has gone to the Southeast. The Southwest (except Mississippi) has higher wage levels and lower rural density; capital-intensive industry becomes relatively more important. Compared to the Southeast, the Southwest has proportionately less than half as much of its employment in the five most labor-intensive industries. This contrast leads to plant location contrasts. Not all differences in significance for the indicators fit the manufacturing differences, but most do.

Population. The first evidence that Southeast-Southwest manufacturing differences affect the significance of growth indicators comes from the population-interval sample, analyzed in chapter 4. Table 4-1 shows that in the Southeast, cities of 5,000 to 10,000 have the highest median growth rate. But in the Southwest, the highest median belongs to cities above 30,000. Though not statistically significant, these findings accord with the manufacturing pattern. Labor-intensive industry (Southeast) seeks low wages and unskilled workers, which it most readily finds in small cities and rural locations. Capital-intensive industry (Southwest) is not overly concerned about wages; it is more prone to seek the skilled labor and amenities of larger cities.

Importance. Further evidence of manufacturing's effect on other indicators comes from the importance ratings. BUSNS and TRADE sometimes have significant partial correlations in the Southeast (only) even when MFG > 0, to which they are related, is held constant; the Southeast's best eleven-variable R (table 14-2) provides an example. And in other situations where MFG > 0 is not controlled, BUSNS and TRADE have more significant partials; the Southeast's best six-variable Rs (table 14-1) are illustrative. A plausible explanation is that business and trade accentuate labor market competition. This deters new labor-intensive manufacturing, found primarily in the Southeast, from locating in the more important cities.

Manufacturing. Naturally, the Southeast-Southwest differences are prominent for manufacturing. Variables that stress labor-intensive manufacturing—the

E_m/E variables—have significantly negative correlations in the Southeast only. This evidently reflects labor-intensive industry's slow growth and its aversion to competitive labor markets. Since the Southwest has comparatively little labor-intensive manufacturing, this effect is confined to the Southeast. True, the same logic leads one to expect variables stressing capital-intensive industry—VA/P and MFG—to be significant in the Southwest, whereas they too are significant only in the Southeast. The reason may be that VA/P and MFG measure overall manufacturing, not just the capital-intensive element, except when E_m/E is used to control the labor-intensive element. E_m/E does not work in the Southwest, for there is too little labor-intensive industry to register.

Education. An education variable, SCHOOL (percentage of children in school), has the sharpest Southeast-Southwest contrast in significance. It is negatively correlated with growth in the Southeast, positively correlated in the Southwest— and significant in both subregions. The contrast probably results from the rural orientation of labor-intensive industry in the Southeast and the urban orientation of capital-intensive industry in the Southwest. Rural areas have lower educational levels than urban areas; schooling becomes a proxy for the rural or urban character of the community and for its unskilled (low-wage) or skilled (high-wage) labor.

Wages. Because low wages explain the high proportion of labor-intensive industry found in the Southeast, one expects wages to be better correlated with growth in the Southeast than in the Southwest. In fact, however, the wage variables have higher *simple* correlations in the Southwest. This is largely because racial mix obscures the wage influence in the Southeast; the greater importance of taxes, for which wages is partly a proxy, in the Southwest is also a factor. Hence, the most reliable wage variable—EARN— has a much higher standardized *partial* correlation in the Southeast than in the Southwest, race and property taxes being held constant. Again, EARN supports four of the Southeast's but just one of the Southwest's best multiple correlations.

Property Taxes. The property tax factor is more significant in the Southwest. For example, only the Southwest gives TAX/P a significant simple correlation. Also, the tax factor is less ambiguous in the Southwest: the wage factor is too weak there for TAX/P to be much of a wage proxy. A convincing explanation is that capital-intensive firms—those with heavy investments in taxable plants and equipment—are more concerned about taxes than labor-intensive firms are. Moreover, since low population density and skilled labor requirements make it hard for Southwest firms to locate in rural areas, these firms are more apt to feel the higher tax rates found in urban places. Finding a city with relatively low tax rates (by city standards) is therefore more important in the Southwest.

Metropolitan Areas. The metropolitan variables are significant in the Southwest but not the Southeast. Southwestern cities located close to major metropolitan areas, or located where the nearest metropolis is relatively large or fastgrowing, tend to grow fast. In contrast, partial correlations for the Southeast actually reveal a tendency—almost significant—toward fast growth in the more remote cities. Why the difference? A big segment of southeastern manufacturing—the labor-intensive segment—prefers to locate far from major metropolitan areas. This preference for remote, rural locations, where wages are low, cancels the urban orientation of the capital-intensive segment. Another factor is the smaller proportion of market-oriented (contrasted with labor-oriented) industry in the Southeast. Strong regional markets are less likely in the Southeast to jointly stimulate (common causation) a metropolis and nearby cities.

Residential Amenities: The next Southeast-Southwest difference looks spurious but will be mentioned on the chance that it is part of the pattern. Inconclusive evidence suggests that residential amenities may enhance growth in the Southeast. If so, this might be because the Southeast has more variation in the housing offered by those cities with locational potential. Such variation could arise if new plants went to both rural (labor-intensive plants) and urban (capital-intensive plants) places in the Southeast but mainly to urban places in the Southwest. The urban places might almost all have acceptable housing, while many rural places did not. Residential amenities would then be significant only in that region—the Southeast—where appreciable amounts of new industry went to rural locations.

Prior Growth and Migration. Prior population growth and prior net migration are both good indicators for the Southwest but less useful in the Southeast. Labor-oriented manufacturing in the Southeast again seems responsible. Cities that grew in the 1950–60 decade thereby acquired more competitive labor markets. This effect was stronger in the Southeast—all the more so because the labor-oriented plants were locating in small towns where the labor supplies were small to begin with. And new 1960–70 plants, being more labor-oriented in the Southeast, were more deterred by recent growth in the Southeast than in the Southwest. Where migration is concerned, the Southeast's high rural population density further weakens the indicator. Because the migration variable uses county data, rural out-migration to metropolitan areas can offset urban in-migration in the Southeast.

Unemployment. Finally, the unemployment rate is a good indicator in just one region, this time the Southeast. Southeastern cities with high unemployment tend not to grow. Why not southwestern cities too? Possibly because the Southwest has more capital-intensive industry. This industry is more prone to cyclical changes in unemployment. The 1960–70 period was one of modest recovery from unemployment. Southwestern cities with high 1960 unemployment probably had more growth of the type that comes from economic recovery. Recovery-type growth could have neutralized out-migration by the unemployed. In the Southeast, where unemployment is more apt to be non-cyclical, recovery-type growth was perhaps less common.

17 Application: Predicting Growth

The findings and conclusions of this study can be applied to the problem of predicting growth in nonmetropolitan cities. Toward this end, two scoring formulas—one for the Southeast and one for the Southwest—have been devised. These evaluate the growth potential of each city in the over-10,000 sample. A city's evaluation, or score, rests on its status with respect to factors found to be significant. Both formulas are remarkably effective in discriminating between fast-growing and slow-growing cities: in both regions, 28 of 29 fast cities but only 1 of 29 slow cities exceed a critical (cutoff) score. This performance indicates that the formulas would probably discriminate with reasonable accuracy for a later period.

General Technique

The problem is to predict growth, not in a precise quantitative sense but in a discriminant sense: we want to predict which cities are likely or unlikely to experience relatively fast growth. Various methods could be used for discriminating between fast and slow cities. The most obvious are mathematical discriminant functions, multiple regression equations, and weighted scoring systems.

Mathematical functions and regression equations were ruled out largely on grounds of complexity. Particularly where the more sophisticated forms of discriminant analysis are concerned, computers and technical expertise are necessary. Many local economic development planning groups do not have the trained statisticians needed to operate regression and other models. Furthermore, nontechnically oriented planning directors and community leaders often view such "mathematical models" with skepticism (sometimes justifiable): techniques beyond the ken of those who must agree to their use can be at a severe disadvantage when competing with simpler but understandable systems. What is needed is a technique that is simple enough to explain to planners, businessmen, and political leaders yet that is empirically based and can predict as well as a good statistical model.

The above considerations, particularly the desire for simplicity, governed the choice of a weighted scoring system for predicting fast or slow growth. A scoring system for cities is comparable to the rating system for factors in chapter 15. But with cities, points are awarded for factors (e.g., air service) instead of for statistical measures such as chi-square. The new scoring system is weighted in the sense that different factors may carry different point maximums (weights). Thus, in the formula for the Southeast, unemployment carries up to seven points, highways up to six, wages up to four, and value added up to two. Points are summed for each city. The total, or score, becomes a criterion for predicting growth.

The design of each scoring formula entailed six steps: (1) assigning each variable a preliminary weight based on its importance, as judged from table 15-4, (2) dividing the range of values for each variable into intervals, comparable and often identical to those used in the chi-square analyses, (3) assigning point values for each interval, (4) scoring each city in the over-10,000 sample according to these initial values, (5) determining the cutoff score that best discriminated between fast and slow cities, and (6) refining the weights, intervals, and point values to raise the relative scores of fast cities to above-cutoff levels and lower the relative scores of slow cities to below-cutoff levels. In this process, some variables were dropped and others added to enhance predictive reliability.

The more important indicators received initial point ranges of zero to six; the less important ones had lower maximums. Where findings justified fewer intervals than points, intervals were not created for all possible point values from zero to the maximum. Refinements resulted from trial-and-error experimentation. In appropriate situations, relative instead of absolute indicators were used, as in some of the chi-square tables. Two indicators benefited from a combination of absolute and relative intervals. Two others, MFG and VA, gave maximum value to both the highest and the lowest intervals to reflect a U-shaped curve relating manufacturing to growth.

Racial mix would have been a useful indicator but was not used. The decision to leave it out cannot be defended on scientific grounds. But if forecasts are to be used in allocating economic assistance, it seems unwise and contrary to egalitarian goals to penalize the relatively black cities.

The Southeast Formula

The Southeast scoring formula uses eleven indicators. Ranked here by weight in the formula, with the basic variables indicated in parentheses, these are the unemployment rate (UNEMP), Interstate highways (HWY), air service (AIR), colleges (COL-5), prior growth (G:50-60), property taxes (TAX/P), labor-intensive manufacturing (E_m/E), wages (EARN), nonmanufacturing cities and capital-intensive manufacturing (MFG and VA), and schooling (SCHOOL).

Intervals and Points. The classification intervals and point values for these indicators are as follows:

Indicator Intervals	*Points*

UNEMP: 1960 Unemployment Rate

3% (absolute) or less	7
2% or more below state median	5
1% below state median	3
Equal to state median	2
1% above state median	1
2% or more above state median	0

HWY: Miles to Interstate Interchange

0–5 miles	6
6 miles	5
7–8 miles	4
9–10 miles	3
11–12 miles	2
13–15 miles	1
Over 15 miles	0

AIR: Miles to Commercial Airport

0–15 miles	6
16–25 miles	5
26–30 miles	4
31–35 miles	3
36–40 miles	2
41–50 miles	1
Over 50 miles	0

COL-5: College Status

Graduate school	6
Four-year college	4
No college	0

G:50–60: Prior Growth Rate

20% or more	6
18–19%	5
15–17%	4
10–14%	3
5–9%	2
0–4%	1
Negative	0

TAX/P: Property Taxes per Capita

$20 or more below state median	6
$6 to $19 below state median	5
$3 to $5 below state median	4
Within $2 of state median	3
$3 above state median	2
$4 to $19 above state median	1
$20 or more above state median	0

E_m/E: Percent Employed in Manufacturing

15% or less	6
16–20%	5
21–25%	4
26–30%	3
31–35%	2

Indicator Intervals	*Points*
E_m/E: Percent Employed in Manufacturing	
36–40%	1
Over 40%	0
EARN: Median Annual Earnings (Operatives)	
$500 or more below state median	4
$200 to $499 below state median	3
Within $199 of state median	2
$200 to $499 above state median	1
$500 or more above state median	0
MFG: Rand McNally Manufacturing Rating	
3 (Mm)	3
2 (Mx)	2
1 (Xm)	0
0 (Xx)	3
VA: Manufacturing Value Added	
Over $30 million	2
$25 to $29 million	1
$5 to $24 million	0
Under $5 million	1
SCHOOL: Percentage of Children in School	
Under 85%	2
85% or more	0

It bears repeating that the medians used with those variables that have relative rather than absolute intervals are the state (not subregional) medians for all sample cities (fast-moderate-slow, over 10,000) in the state. Thus each city is classified by the norm for its state, and different cities may use different medians. (These state medians should not be confused with a different sort of median used to measure earnings with EARN—namely, median earnings for individual workers in particular cities.)

The data sources and substantive descriptions for the eleven variables are given in chapter 2.

Formula Validity. Is the Southeast formula a valid tool for discriminating between fast and slow cities? Strictly speaking, a predictive formula should be validated with new data—a new group of cases (cross-validation) or the same cases in a later period. Unfortunately, this is not possible. Nearly all of the Southeast's fast and slow (i.e., top and bottom one-third in growth rate) cities were used up in calibrating the formula. As for the over-5,000 sample, it contains most of the same cities and lacks data for some indicators. Cities from another region would not provide a good test, for the formula is not designed for other regions. And, of course, a later-period test is impossible before the 1980 census is published.

A very tentative sort of validation is nevertheless possible. It entails, first,

Figure 17-1
Southeast: Comparative Predictive Score Distributions[a]

Score	Fast Cities	Slow Cities	Moderate Cities
41–42	*		
39–40	* * *		
37–38	*		*
35–36	* *		
33–34	*		*
31–32	* * * * * * *		* * * *
29–30	* * * * * *	*	
27–28	* * * * * * *		* * * *
Cutoff Score -(27)			
25–26		* * *	* * * *
23–24	*	* * * * * * * *	* * * * * *
21–22		* * * * *	* * * *
19–20		* * * *	*
17–18		* * * * *	* * *
15–16		* *	
13–14			*
12		*	
Median	31	22	24

[a]Each asterisk represents one city.

evaluating the formula's results for the fifty-eight cities used to calibrate the formula (this is loosely comparable to an R^2 test) and, second, testing the formula with the twenty-nine moderate-growth cities.

Figure 17-1 compares the scores for the twenty-nine fast and twenty-nine slow cities in the over-10,000 sample. The fast cities show generally high scores, the slow cities generally low scores. The optimal cutoff score—the minimum "passing" score that best discriminates between fast and slow—is 27. Only one fast city fails to pass; only one slow city passes. The highest score for a fast city, 42, is well above the highest for a slow city, 30. The lowest "fast" score, 24, is double the lowest "slow" score, 12.

The two prediction errors relate to colleges. Americus, Georgia, is the fast city that fails to pass. It has a college—Georgia Southwestern—but for technical reasons was scored as a noncollege city: the college fell below the 1,000 enrollment level used as a cutoff for the bachelor's degree category. Nevertheless, enrollment went from 519 in 1960 to 2,383 in 1970—a 359 percent relative increase and a 1,864 absolute increase. The absolute increase compares with Americus's population increase of 2,619 for the decade. On the slow side, Orangeburg, South Carolina, is the slow city with the passing score. It is the one college city in the basic sample that failed to exhibit fast growth.

The twenty-nine moderate-growth cities from the augmented sample have growth rates lower than those of the fast cities but higher than those of the

slow cities. If the formula is valid, the moderate cities should score generally
below the fast cities but above the slow ones. One cannot assume, though,
that the moderates should average exactly halfway between fast and slow.
Conceivably, the moderate cities more nearly resemble the fast cities, or the
slow. In fact, since growth rates are skewed toward the high side, the average
growth rate for the moderate cities is closer to that for the slow ones than
that for the fast. Hence, a reasonable hypothesis would be that the moderate
cities are closer to the slow than to the fast ones in their scores.

And they are. Figure 17-1 shows, first of all, that the moderate-city
scores average below the fast scores and above the slow ones—which is what
formula validity requires. They also tend to be closer to the slow ones. Thus
we find twenty-eight fast cities with passing scores, ten moderate cities, and
one slow city. The top fast score is 42, the top moderate score 37, and the
top slow score 30. The lowest scores are fast, 24; moderate, 13; and slow, 12.
The medians are 31, 24, and 22.

Adjustments for 1970-80. Before using the Southeast formula to predict for
1970-80, it would be necessary or advisable to make certain adjustments.
Some of these are required by changes in the general magnitudes of certain
indicators; others are simply matters of judgment.

One type of adjustment involves those indicators whose intervals were
defined in terms of the medians for sample cities. The indicators are UNEMP,
TAX/P, and EARN. Their 1960 state medians, used in calibrating the formula,
were based on all sample cities (fast, moderate, and slow). For median purposes, all sample cities is a close approximation to all non-SMSA cities above
10,000 population; only a few such cities were left out. (These variously were
too close to other cities, had growth rates too low for the fast group, or had
growth rates too high for the slow group.) The "left out" cities are unlikely to
be unrepresentative of cities in general in their unemployment, tax, and earnings levels. Hence, the 1970 medians needed to predict for 1970-80 could
include them. However, SMSA cities, including suburbs, should still be left out.

VA is another relatively dynamic variable with a changing base level. The
formula uses 1958 VA, taken from the *1958 Census of Manufactures*. But predictions for 1970-80 would have to use the 1967 census. And the intervals
would have to be adjusted for price inflation. The BLS *Consumer Price Index*
reads 86.6 for 1958 and 100.0 for 1967. On this basis, the "Over $30 million"
interval becomes "Over $35 million," "$25 to $29 million" becomes "$30 to
$34 million," and "Under $5 million" becomes "Under $6 million."

The intervals for TAX/P, set to fit the 1960 data, are somewhat irregular
in width. For 1970, it would be reasonable to judgmentally adjust the cutoff
between the five-point and the four-point interval and that between the two-
point and the one-point interval.

It was observed in chapter 7 that the college factor will probably be less
important in the 1970s—because the population structure and the Vietnam war

led to abnormally high enrollment increases in the 1960s. How much colleges should be down-weighted is a matter of conjecture. But, to judge by the U.S. Office of Education projections presented earlier, it appears sensible to cut the 6-4-0 point structure back to 2-1-0. This would have virtually no effect on the slow scores and would not require any lowering of the cutoff scores.

Finally, all 1960 values for indicators should be replaced with 1970 values, and the prior growth indicator (G:50–60) should substitute 1960–70 growth for 1950–60 growth.

The Southwest Formula

The scoring formula for the Southwest uses twelve indicators: prior growth (G:50–60), air service (AIR), colleges (COL-5), property taxes (TAX/P), SMSA distance (D_m), the unemployment rate (UNEMP), prior migration (MIGR), Interstate highways (HWY), wages (EARN), manufacturing (VA and MFG), and schooling (SCHOOL). The new variables—not used in the Southeast formula—are MIGR and D_m, but SCHOOL has undergone a change (awarding points for high instead of low schooling) that makes it substantively a new variable. E_m/E, used in the Southeast formula, is dropped.

Intervals and Points. The twelve indicators use the following classification intervals and point values:

Indicator Intervals	Points
G:50–60: Prior Growth Rate	
50% or more	8
40% to 49%	7
2% above state median to 39% absolute	6
Within 1% of state median	5
2% or 3% below state median, over 4% absolute	4
4% or 5% below state median, over 4% absolute	3
6% below state median, over 4% absolute	2
0% to 4%	1
Negative	0
AIR: Miles to Commercial Airport	
0–15 miles	6
16–25 miles	5
26–30 miles	4
31–35 miles	3
36–40 miles	2
41–50 miles	1
Over 50 miles	0
COL-5: College Status	
Graduate school	6
Four-year college	4
No college	0

Indicator Intervals	*Points*
TAX/P: Property Taxes per Capita	
$8 or more below state median	6
$5 to $7 below state median	5
$2 to $4 below state median	4
Within $1 of state median	3
$2 to $4 above state median	2
$5 to $7 above state median	1
$8 or more above state median	0
D_m: Distance to Nearest Major SMSA	
160 miles or less	6
161–175 miles	2
Over 175 miles	0
UNEMP: 1960 Unemployment Rate	
3% absolute or less	5
1% or more below state median but above 3%	3
Equal to state median	2
1% above state median	1
2% or more above state median	0
MIGR: Prior Net Migration	
+6% or more	3
Less than +6%	0
HWY: Miles to Interstate Interchange	
0–8 miles	2
9–15 miles	1
Over 15 miles	0
EARN: Median Annual Earnings (Operatives)	
$200 or more below state median	2
Within $199 of state median	1
$200 or more above state median	0
VA: Manufacturing Value Added	
$0 to $4 million	2
$5 million or more	0
SCHOOL: Percentage of Children in School	
90% or more	2
82–89%	1
81% or less	0
MFG: Rand McNally Manufacturing Rating	
0 (Xx)	1
1 (Xm, Mx, Mm)	0

The two manufacturing indicators, VA and MFG, are used differently here than in the Southeast formula. In that formula, both follow the concept of a U-shaped curve relating manufacturing to growth: they credit cities for ultra-low manufacturing levels and for high levels of capital-intensive manufacturing. The Southwest formula, however, uses VA and MFG only to identify non-manufacturing cities.

Figure 17–2
Southwest: Comparative Predictive Score Distributions[a]

Score	Fast Cities	Slow Cities	Moderate Cities
40–41	*		
38–39			
36–37			
34–35	* * *		
32–33	* * * *		
30–31	* * * *	*	* *
28–29	* * *		* * *
26–27	* * * * * * * * * *		* * * *
24–25	* * *		* * * * * *
Cutoff Score - (24)			
22–23		* * * * *	* * *
20–21		* * * * * * * * *	* * * * * *
18–19		* * * * * *	*
16–17	*	* *	* * *
14–15		* *	*
12–13		* *	
10–11		* *	
Median	29	20	24

[a]Each asterisk represents one city.

Formula Validity. Figure 17–2 tests the validity of the Southwest formula by comparing the scores of the twenty-nine fast and twenty-nine slow cities in the Southwest sample. It also cross-validates by asking whether the moderate-city scores generally fall between those of the fast and those of the slow cities. As before, these tests are tentative.

Again, the formula appears valid. The fast cities show a strong tendency to outscore the slow ones. When the passing score is set at 24, only one fast city fails to pass and only one slow city does pass. The highest "fast" score, 41, compares with a top "slow" score of 31. The lowest "fast" score is 16, which compares with a low "slow" score of 10.

As in the Southeast, the two erroneous predictions relate to colleges. The fast city that does not pass—Levelland, Texas—is a college city that was scored as a noncollege city because the college's enrollment was below 1,000. South Plains College is the school. Its enrollment rose from 478 in 1960 to 1,711 in 1970—a 258 percent relative increase and a 1,233 absolute increase. The 1,233 figure almost equals Levelland's 1,292 population increase for 1960–70; and a proportional increase in college faculty and administrative employment could easily account for the difference of 59 persons. Among the slow cities, Magnolia, Arkansas, is the one with the passing score. It is one of two college cities in the Southwest that had slow growth.

Although the moderate cities remain unsatisfactory for any thoroughgoing cross-validation, they continue to provide at least tentative conclusions about the formula's validity. Validity requires that the moderate cities score somewhere between the fast and the slow ones. The chart shows that they do. The median scores are 29 for the fast cities, 24 for the moderates, and 20 for the slow ones. The highest scores are fast, 41; moderate, 30; and slow 31 (the only instance where slow outscored moderate). The lowest scores are fast, 16; moderate, 14; and slow, 10. Passing scores are attained by twenty-eight fast cities, fifteen moderates, and one slow city.

Adjustments for 1970–80. To use the Southeast formula for predicting 1970–80 growth, the same types of adjustments discussed in connection with the Southeast formula would be necessary. New state medians would have to be computed for G:50-60, TAX/P, UNEMP, and EARN. A new cutoff point for VA would again be needed. College status should again be downgraded as an indicator, probably to a 2-1-0 point structure. All 1960 values should give way to 1970 values, and 1950-60 changes should be replaced by 1960-70 changes.

The Why and Wherefore of Growth

The findings of this and the preceding chapters confirm that growth is more than a random phenomenon. It has many causes, undoubtedly including some that were not examined. (The unexamined causes include local entrepreneurship, the growth and decline of military bases and other government installations, centralness of location within market regions, proximity to resources, tourist attractions, local promotion, labor union activity, and extraordinary annexations.) Not all cities grow—or fail to grow—for the same reasons. But by treating growth as being additive—as having multiple causes that add incrementally to a total—one can fairly accurately explain why some cities grow fast and others grow slowly.

Index

About the Author

Leonard F. Wheat is an economist with the Economic Development Administration of the U.S. Department of Commerce. He has also held positions with the Office of Regional Development Planning, the Bureau of the Budget, the Navy Department's Office of Special Projects, and the Minnesota Department of Taxation. He received the B.A. from the University of Minnesota, Duluth, in 1952, the M.A.P.A. (public administration) from the University of Minnesota in 1954, and the Ph.D. in political economy and government from Harvard University in 1958. Dr. Wheat is the author of an earlier economic study, *Regional Growth and Industrial Location;* a philosophical study, *Paul Tillich's Dialectical Humanism;* and research monographs dealing with the impact of highways and air service on manufacturing growth in cities. His affiliations include the American Economic Association, the American Society for Public Administration, the Society of Government Economists, and numerous conservation organizations.